ROUTLEDGE LIBRARY EDITIONS: EDUCATION MANAGEMENT

Volume 20

THE POLITICS OF REORGANIZING SCHOOLS

THE POLITICS OF REORGANIZING SCHOOLS

STEWART RANSON

LONDON AND NEW YORK

First published in 1990 by Allen & Unwin

This edition first published in 2018
by Routledge
2 Park Square, Milton Park, Abingdon, Oxon OX14 4RN

and by Routledge
711 Third Avenue, New York, NY 10017

Routledge is an imprint of the Taylor & Francis Group, an informa business

© 1990 Stewart Ranson

All rights reserved. No part of this book may be reprinted or reproduced or utilised in any form or by any electronic, mechanical, or other means, now known or hereafter invented, including photocopying and recording, or in any information storage or retrieval system, without permission in writing from the publishers.

Trademark notice: Product or corporate names may be trademarks or registered trademarks, and are used only for identification and explanation without intent to infringe.

British Library Cataloguing in Publication Data
A catalogue record for this book is available from the British Library

ISBN: 978-1-138-48720-8 (Set)
ISBN: 978-1-351-04158-4 (Set) (ebk)
ISBN: 978-1-138-48798-7 (Volume 20) (hbk)
ISBN: 978-1-351-04074-7 (Volume 20) (ebk)

Publisher's Note
The publisher has gone to great lengths to ensure the quality of this reprint but points out that some imperfections in the original copies may be apparent.

Disclaimer
The publisher has made every effort to trace copyright holders and would welcome correspondence from those they have been unable to trace.

KEY ISSUES IN EDUCATION

Series Editor:
Dr Robert Burgess, *University of Warwick*

The Politics of Reorganizing Schools

Stewart Ranson

with Kieron Walsh in chapter 3
Institute of Local Government Studies

London
UNWIN HYMAN
Boston Sydney Wellington

© Stewart Ranson 1990

This book is copyright under the Berne Convention. No reproduction without permission. All rights reserved.

Published by the Academic Division of
Unwin Hyman Ltd
15/17 Broadwick Street, London W1V 1FP, UK

Unwin Hyman Inc.,
8 Winchester Place, Winchester, Mass. 01890, USA

Allen & Unwin (Australia) Ltd,
8 Napier Street, North Sydney, NSW 2060, Australia

Allen & Unwin (New Zealand) Ltd in association with the
Port Nicholson Press Ltd,
Compusales Building, 75 Ghuznee Street, Wellington 1, New Zealand

First published in 1990

British Library Cataloguing in Publication Data

Ranson, Stewart, 1946–
 The politics of reorganizing schools. (Key issues in education)
 1. England. Education. Reorganisation
 I. Title. II. Walsh, Kieron
 379.1'52
 ISBN 0–04–370196–5
   0–04–370197–3

Library of Congress Cataloging-in-Publication Data

Ranson, Stewart.
 The politics of reorganizing schools / Stewart Ranson : with Kieron Walsh in chapter 3.
  p. cm. – (Key issues in education)
 Includes bibliographical references.
 ISBN 0–04–370196–5. – ISBN 0–04–370197–3 (pbk.)
 1. High school enrollment – Great Britain. 2. Education and state – Great Britain. 3. Politics and education – Great Britain. 4. Education. Secondary – England – Manchester – Case studies.
 I. Walsh, Kieron. II. Title. III. Series.
 LC146.8.G7R36 1989   89–38423
 373.12'1941–dc   CIP

Disc conversion in 10/11 Garamond Book ITC by Columns of Reading
and printed by Billing and Sons Ltd., Worcester

Contents

Series editor's preface		xi
Foreword		xiii
1	Understanding the implications of falling rolls	1
2	The challenge from central government	10
3	LEA strategies for institutional reorganization	25
4	Reorganizing schools in Manchester: a case study	49
5	Analysing the changing politics and government of reorganizations	87
6	Public policy for the future	107
Guide to reading		123
References		124
Index		131

For
Dudley Fiske and Edward Simpson
In the service of public education

Series editor's preface

Each volume in the *Key Issues in Education* series is designed to provide a concise authoritative guide to a topic of current concern to teachers, researchers and educational policy makers. The books in the series comprise an introduction to some of the key debates in the contemporary practice of education. In particular, each author demonstrates how the social sciences can help us to analyse, explain and understand educational issues. The books in the series review key debates, and the authors complement this material by making detailed reference to their own research, which helps to illustrate the way research evidence in the social sciences and education can contribute to our understanding of educational policy and practice.

All the contributors to this series have extensive experience of their chosen field and have worked with teachers and other educational personnel. The volumes have been written to appeal to students who are intending to become teachers, working teachers who seek to familiarize themselves with new research and research evidence, as well as social scientists who are engaged in the study of education. Each author seeks to make educational research and debate accessible to those engaged in the practice of education. At the end of each volume there is a short guide to further reading for those who wish to pursue the topic in greater depth. The series provides a comprehensive guide to contemporary issues in education and demonstrates the importance of social science research for understanding educational practice.

In recent years, there has been much debate about the implications of falling school rolls for students, teachers and

The Politics of Reorganizing Schools

schools. Stewart Ranson and Kieron Walsh bring together some of their research on the effect of falling rolls on the politics and government of education. The issues examined include school closure, amalgamation and the replacement of sixth forms with tertiary colleges, as well as the implications of these activities for the curriculum, staffing, organization and management of local education. A series of rich insights are provided on the politics of reorganizing schools through the case study of Manchester. In short, this book makes an authoritative contribution to our understanding of how the politics of education affects the policy and practice of reorganizing schools.

Robert Burgess
University of Warwick

Foreword

The sharp fall in the birth rate in the late 1960s has led to a period of contraction of school rolls that will last into the 1990s. Declining rolls together with the contraction in public expenditure on education has had considerable repercussions for the government and management of the education service. The curriculum, staffing and organization of schools as well as the management style of local education authorities have all been affected fundamentally.

The focus of this book is upon the implications of falling school rolls for the institutional organization of secondary schools: whether schools should be closed or amalgamated and whether a new system of post-16 colleges would appropriately replace the school sixth form. These controversial policy issues, which illuminate sharply the changing government and politics of education, form the substance of this book.

Chapter 1 begins with the several dimensions of contextual change which the education service has experienced and considers the implications raised for educational policy and the organization of government. An analytical framework is introduced to aid understanding and explanation of the changing pattern of politics and government of reorganization.

In chapter 2 the response of central government to the institutional implications of falling rolls is considered. Both Labour and Conservative administrations confronted the dilemma of 'surplus capacity': of wanting to reduce school places in order to save scarce public resources in a time of expenditure cuts, but also to seize the political opportunity to use spare capacity in order to offer parents more choice of school. In the early 1980s the government attempted to ease the tension but the recent 1988 Education Reform Act has favoured the politics of parental choice.

Chapters 3 and 4 explore the implications of falling rolls for the LEAs, the institutional alternatives they have considered and the political processes which reorganization planning has encouraged. A detailed case study is presented of the politics of reorganization in one local authority, Manchester, which because it was perceived as the prototype for local planning, embraced national as well as local politics.

The pattern of politics and government of institutional reorganization which has emerged in the 1980s is analysed in chapter 5. It is very different from previous periods of reorganization since the Second World War, such as the establishing of secondary schools, and comprehensive reorganization in the 1960s. Whereas in the 1960s there was partnership between central and local government with initiative often resting with the professionals, the 1980s has seen more conflict between the tiers of government, greater ministerial dominance and a new assertiveness from parental interest groups. The issue of institutional reorganization can provide a case study of more general patterns in the changing government of education. In the final chapter the issues of policy involved in institutional reorganization are reviewed and a form of government appropriate to the task of reorganising schools is proposed.

This book has developed from research and teaching at the Institute. I was part of a team funded by SSRC (as the ESRC then was) during 1979–82 to study the changing forms of policy planning between central and local government. My focus was upon the impact of contraction on the politics and government of educational planning (curricular and institutional provision) for 16- to 19-year-olds. A series of seminars in the early 1980s on falling school rolls used contributions from the DES, LEA councillors and officers, headteachers and parent representatives. In 1981 the institute won a grant from the DES to study the management of the teaching force. This research, led by Kieron Walsh, involved a study of Birmingham which it is appropriate to incorporate in the analysis of this book.

I am grateful to the ESRC and the DES for funding the research upon which this book is based. I also wish to thank Bob Morris, John Stewart and Tim Whitaker for reading earlier drafts of the book and offering searching critical comments.

Foreword

Kieron Walsh has been especially helpful, contributing the study of Birmingham and transforming many clumsy expressions into intelligible prose. I am grateful to Bob Burgess for the invitation to write this book and for his unfailing patience and support. Dot Woolley, Di Myers and Lynn Dixon have at times had the unenviable task of typing the chapters and coped admirably. Helena Ranson has put up with the irritation of distant word processing while preparing for the more important educational task of serving with distinction disadvantaged young adults in Coventry schools. The flaws that clearly remain are of course not attributable to those who have given their support.

Stewart Ranson
Coventry, September, 1988

Chapter 1

Understanding the implications of falling rolls

No sooner had many local education authorities implemented a scheme of comprehensive education in the 1960s or early 1970s, than they were forced to contemplate a further period of reorganizing their schools and colleges. By the late 1970s a number of LEAs began to appreciate the scale of the falling birth rate and the effect it would have upon their school rolls; for some, the prospect was that by 1990 they would not have enough pupils to fill half their existing schools. Change was inevitable, yet the issue of what to do with 'surplus capacity' in schools generated a number of controversies which form the subject of this book. I shall describe the changed context before clarifying the significant questions raised for the politics and government of education.

The changing context

Education was the fastest growing service, whether in the public or the private sector, between 1955 and 1975 (Cheshire, 1976). A rising birth rate, economic growth and political will coalesced in the expansion of the education service during this period. After the Second World War LEAs had to build more schools to provide for the growing school population. The emphasis upon expanding educational opportunities led, in the 1960s, to a programme of institutional reform: grammar schools and secondary modern schools were to be reorganized into non-selective comprehensive schools which would provide all pupils with equal opportunity to develop their potential (cf. David, 1977; Kogan, 1978; James,

1980). A widespread belief in the benefit of education to society and the economy provided the rationale for the expansion of the service.

The same forces which led to the expansion of education turned, from the mid 1970s, into forces of contraction. A declining birth rate and the prospect of falling school rolls, the economic recession and the ensuing public expenditure cuts, together with growing disquiet about the achievement of the service, all combined to produce a more severe context for education:

FALLING SCHOOL ROLLS

The birth rate fell by about one third between 1964 and 1977, and has risen only slightly since then. The implications for the numbers of pupils in school have been dramatic: the school population which grew to a peak of 9 million in 1977 (from 5 million in 1946) will decline perhaps to below 7 million by 1990. Primary school numbers peaked in 1973, then fell by about 30 per cent before beginning to rise again in the mid-1980s, while secondary numbers peaked in 1980 at 4.1 million and will fall to 2.8 million in 1991. Although it was known that the birth rate would increase again, demographic predictions in the early 1980s did not anticipate rapid growth nor, therefore, the prospect of great increases in school rolls before the next century is well advanced.

LEA planners, moreover, could not expect the spare places in their schools to be filled with increasing numbers of young people deciding to stay on into the sixth form. In the late 1970s, the 'staying on rate' was relatively static or even falling, while those choosing to go to further education college were increasing and, as youth unemployment grew, those young people who used to leave school for work were choosing to (or constrained to) join the new training schemes rather than stay on into the sixth form.

EXPENDITURE CUTS

The recession, stimulated by the 1973 Middle East War, led in due course to rolling programmes of cuts in public expenditure and local authority spending in particular. The elaborate machinery of expenditure controls on local authorities —

The context

targets, rate caps, penalties and so on – were designed necessarily to reduce education (60 per cent of local government) as well as other social services. When Peston (1982) and Stewart (1983) analysed the value of rate support grant in 'real' terms (what money will buy taking into account inflation) they revealed substantial cuts in allocated expenditure. The constraints on local government expenditure have grown more severe in the 1980s.

Year by year HM Inspectorate, in its annual reports on the effects of expenditure policies on education, have illustrated the impacts of cuts: 'many schools are finding it increasingly difficult to replace old books, equipment and furniture, to implement curricular change, and to respond to planned changes in assessment and examination procedures' (HMI, 1986). This toll of cuts on the learning experiences of young people in schools is graphically chronicled in Hewton's (1986) *Education in Recession*. He finds, in a study on one shire county, that there have been severe cut-backs at all levels in the school system, with implications for morale and the quality of teaching.

The Conservative government claims, properly, that educational spending per pupil has risen since it took power in 1979. The implied contradiction between cuts and growth can be understood if the assumptions upon which the government bases its grant are made explicit. The government's expenditure plans assume that local authorities have removed 'surplus' provision (i.e. teachers) and capacity (i.e. school places). But most LEAs have often not wanted, nor been able, either to close schools or reduce their teaching forces at the pace required to show an 'efficient' relationship between finance and provision. Cuts in other areas of expenditure, therefore, were inescapable. The need to cut has also been reinforced by the higher rate of inflation amongst educational goods and services.

DISQUIET AT THE PERFORMANCE OF EDUCATION

The period of educational growth was fuelled by great expectations of the service. But during the 1970s there was growing concern about whether those ambitions were being achieved. Were standards of achievement and behaviour falling, was the curriculum relevant to all children and were they being adequately prepared for the transition from school to work? Were teachers properly accountable to parents and the community as well as the LEA, or had they become a professional enclave cut off from the community?

At the centre of much of the debate about structure and performance was the ingrained distinction between school (academic learning) and further education college (vocational training and preparation). Since the mid 1970s both Labour and Conservative Parties as well as the Department of Education (DES) and local authority associations (LAAs) have increasingly questioned the relevance of this curricular and institutional distinction. The Macfarlane Committee, established in 1980 to examine the organization of post-16 education, concluded by recommending 'a reduction in the differences between schools and further education' (DES, 1980, p.36). The debate has focused upon the purpose and form of the change: whether to redirect the learning of young people towards the needs of industry and employment (cf. MSC, 1984) or to widen curricular choice and thus expand educational opportunity as an extension of the comprehensive revolution (Hargreaves, 1984; Pring, 1984; Ranson, Taylor and Brighouse, 1986).

THE NECESSITY OF CHANGE

It is possible, though unlikely, that if rolls alone had changed the service could have adjusted without altering its forward stride. But the juxtaposition of so many elements of transformation and challenge meant that change in the way the service operated was inevitable. As Dudley Fiske, the former Chief Education Officer of Manchester, perceived at the time, 'no change was not an option' (Fiske, 1978).

A DES/LAAs working party was set up in 1976 to examine the implications of falling rolls for buildings and costs, and LEA leaders made speeches calling for action at national and local level (Association of Metropolitan Authorities (AMA) Education Committee, 1976; Fiske, 1977; Newsam, 1978a and b; Briault, 1978).

What action should follow to deal with the surplus capacity that arose from falling school rolls was, however, a contentious issue and gave rise to a number of questions and controversies.

The context

The questions raised

The changed context forced LEAs to review their provision of education, the number and organization of schools and the curriculum provided in schools and colleges. These issues raised a number of controversial questions – about public policy, about education policy and about the organization of government – some of which had been at the centre of educational politics in the post-war period.

The first set of questions focused upon major **issues of public policy**: what should be done with the spare capacity in schools created by falling rolls? The economic value of efficient use of public resources suggested an urgent need to rationalize surplus places in order to release scarce public funds for alternative uses – perhaps for the elderly and their growing need for care and sheltered accommodation. Value for money suggested a programme of school closure and amalgamation (cf. Bailey, 1981, 1984). Yet political values on the other hand could suggest that spare capacity might provide an opportunity for parents to exercise their right to choose a school. This would also strengthen the public accountability of schools. The competing claims of rationalization and parental choice generated a growing controversy (cf. Dennison, 1983).

Falling rolls raised questions about a number of **educational policies**. The local education authority would have to review its commitment to the values of providing educational opportunities to all young people. It would have to ask what curriculum should be offered in each school to support such opportunities and what size of school was needed to justify the staffing of this curriculum (cf. Walsh *et al.*, 1984, 1985). These questions required an LEA to consider whether the quality of education provided in any individual school depended upon managing all the schools as an interdependent system.

Further questions about education policy focused upon the organization of learning and asked 'What kind of school will provide the best education for its pupils?' Falling rolls caused three aspects of this question to be raised: the relationship of institutions to the organization of ability, age and the curriculum:

(i) Should schools remain 'comprehensive'? Does a good education depend upon children of differing abilities and social backgrounds being educated together or separately? Should schools be specialized according to ability?

(ii) Should schools retain small ('uneconomic') sixth forms? Does a good education depend upon young adults (aged 16-19) being educated with, or separately from, younger pupils? Is education any longer 'a good schooling'? Should schools be specialized according to age?

(iii) Should schools be 'academic' while colleges are 'vocational'? Does a good education depend upon separating out kinds of learning between different types of institution or integrating the curricular opportunities, especially for young adults? Should schools be specialized according to the curriculum?

A third and connected set of questions raised by falling rolls and institutional change has been about decision-making procedure. There has been concern over how decisions are arrived at as well as what they are. These are **questions about government** and administration: about what form of political structure and system of public administration would result in the best education for young people. Three issues have been central to decision-making over school reorganizations:

(i) What should be the **organization** of duties and responsibilities in relation to reorganizations?

(ii) Who should be involved in decision-making? What should be the balance of **power** and influence between Whitehall (ministers and officials), Town and County Hall (councillors and officers), teachers, students, their parents and the community?

(iii) How should decisions be arrived at? What **procedures and processes** should be used? Should changes in the system of schools and colleges be planned (and how) or should they emerge from the pattern of choices made by parents and the consumers of the service? Should the public choices which falling rolls required be made by collective decision (through central and local government) or arise out of the private decisions of individuals?

The politics of institutional reorganization provides a case study in the working of the government of education. It offers an opportunity to examine the changing relationship between policy and the organization of government, and to study whether different educational policies about school systems require different administrative procedures and forms of decision-making.

The context

Analysing changing patterns in the government of reorganizations

The questions raised by falling rolls and the transformed context of education led to changes in policy and procedure in the system of government of institutional reorganization.

The analysis depends on the proposition that systems of government are best understood as vehicles of human values and purpose. Its purpose is to explore how the **organization** and procedures of government support or frustrate the values and aims of those who have the power to shape these systems of government (Ranson, Hinings and Greenwood, 1980; Stewart, 1986; Greenwood and Stewart, 1986a).

Since the Second World War there have been three phases of major institutional change in education, each phase illustrating different patterns of values, organization and power in the government of the service:

(i) The phase of establishing a system of tripartite secondary schools: The 1944 Education Act inaugurated a system of universal secondary education committed to the expansion of educational opportunities appropriate to 'age, aptitude and ability'. It became the duty of LEAs to submit development plans for a tripartite system of secondary schools – grammar, technical and modern – for separate cohorts of pupils selected by intelligence test at 11 (this followed the recommendations of the 1943 Norwood Report). The values of differentiated opportunity were to be organized within a 'national service locally administered'.

(ii) The phase of comprehensive reorganization: DES Circular 10/65 requested LEAs to prepare plans to reorganize their selective schools into a comprehensive system which would equalize opportunities for all children. LEAs and teachers gained more discretion in the planning of the new system.

(iii) The phase of falling rolls and post-primary reorganization: Falling rolls in the 1970s and 1980s have necessitated further schemes of amalgamation and reorganization. We shall discuss the growing influence of central government and parents in this phase of reorganization.

The focus of this book is upon clarifying the changing pattern of values, organization and power in this latest phase. Nevertheless comparison with the past will help to illuminate more clearly contemporary patterns in the politics and government of education.

Explaining change

The different phases of institutional reorganization illustrate, it is argued, changes in the system of education government. One analytical task is to clarify the different patterns or types of government as they emerge. Another is to explain why they have changed. To achieve this end a theory of 'the politics of decision-making' is elaborated (cf. Pettigrew, 1973; Burns, 1961; Child, 1972, 1973 in organizational analysis; Kogan, 1978; Archer, 1979, 1981; Salter and Tapper, 1981 in educational policy; Greenwood, Hinings and Ranson, 1977; Saunders 1979 and Dunleavy, 1980 in political studies).

This theory seeks to make sense of the competing strategies of different 'interest groups' within a policy sector. Each group will want the decisions, policies, or plans to reflect their particular values and objectives. To get their way they may have to come into conflict with other groups and the outcome of the struggle will depend upon the relative power of those involved. The key elements in a theory of the politics of decision-making are:

(i) *The actors*: will typically involve defined groups: for example in education – ministers, civil servants, local councillors, officers and advisers, the teachers, parents and community groups. Smaller sections of each of these groups may develop a concern to be involved in a particular issue of policy planning.

(ii) *Motivation and purpose*: Each group may bring to the decision process distinctively different motivations. Each pursues particular aims and objectives, striving to ensure that the relevant decisions embody its 'values' and reflect its 'interests'. We define *values* as those desired ends or preferences which constitute actors' motivations: for some actors these may include seeking the value of equal opportunity, for others the right to individual choice. We define *interests* as the tendency of actors to maintain and enhance their distribution of scarce resources: these may include finance, authority, expertise, information, access, status and many more (cf. Rhodes, 1981; Jones, 1979).

(iii) *Exchange and transactions*: The various groups transact with each other in the struggle to achieve their purposes. Only

The context

by negotiating with the other parties will they be able to gain influence and get their way.

(iv) *Conflict and power*: The divergent purposes and interests of groups may bring them into conflict which can only be resolved in the struggle by those who have more resources and can therefore exact more influence over the decision process. Success in decision-taking reflects relative power. Blau (1964) and Archer (1979) have articulated the conditions necessary for successful accumulation of power: the possession of strategic resources which others may desire; ensuring that they are scarce and unavailable elsewhere; forming alliances and being organized; promoting one's own interests and being indifferent to the resources possessed by others.

This theory makes sense of decision-making by setting policy planning within its political context: identifying combatants, their competing value systems and different bases of power. In the next chapter the strategies of central government administrations since the mid 1970s are explored before, in later chapters, examining the strategies of local authorities.

Chapter 2

The challenge from central government

Declining rolls meant spare places in schools. This presented a financial constraint but also, perhaps, an opportunity to allow parents the possibility of choosing a school for their children. From the late 1970s the challenging conundrum presented to local authorities by central government was to use the opportunity of falling rolls to achieve potentially incompatible purposes: to become more efficient by closing schools, yet at the same time to use the spare capacity to allow more parental choice. Administrators from the department have tended to stress the virtues of rationalization while their ministers, either Labour or Conservative, have wanted both to save resources and make the political gains of granting parents more discretion. Legislation in the 1980s increasingly weighed the balance towards parental choice.

The strategies of rationalization

A number of consultative papers were prepared by the DES between 1978 and 1980 encouraging local authorities to examine systematically 'the problems of rationalization and cost effectiveness' (cf. DES, 1979b, 1979c, 1980). The need for rationalization was expressed most clearly in the Macfarlane Report *Education for 16–19 Year Olds*, which brought together government and local authority association representatives. The overriding strategy of rationalization took a number of interrelated forms, some expressed more explicitly than others:

The challenge

RATIONALISING INSTITUTIONS FOR RESOURCE EFFICENCY

In a period of contracting numbers and financial resources governments have argued that there are important educational as well as financial benefits to be gained by closing or amalgamating schools. The effective management of scarce resources was emphasized by the Macfarlane Committee but had its most forceful expression in DES Circular 2/81, which set out the financial case for removing surplus capacity of accommodation:

> The precise savings to be realized will vary according to local factors. But they will include reductions in heating, lighting and maintenance costs, as well as – for whole schools – teaching, administrative and caretaking costs. Every 100,000 surplus places taken out of use should on average yield savings approaching £10 million – excluding any savings on teachers' salaries. (DES Circular 2/81, p.5)

Not to make such financial savings could only be at the expense of much needed teachers, books and other educational resources. Indeed the circular stressed educational arguments: 'a reduction in the number of permanent places can bring substantial educational benefits'. In secondary schools, closure and amalgamation would protect the curriculum and staffing – HMI (DES 1979a) having demonstrated the way the range of subjects becomes restricted when school size falls to three or four forms of entry; sciences and languages are especially vulnerable. After 16, the disadvantages of small teaching groups become especially acute, and attempts to staff a full range of curricular opportunities is often achieved at the expense of provision in the lower school. There are, the circular maintained, 'powerful arguments in favour of educating 16–19 year olds in fairly large groups' (DES Circular 2/81, p.4).

The government, then, was arguing that rationalization of institutional provision would offer economies of scale that would not only yield financial savings and the realization of capital assets but would also help significantly to maintain and improve the educational effectiveness of schools.

These arguments have been reinforced consistently in government statements (most recently in DES Circular 3/87) and by the Audit Commission in its reports, including *Towards Better Management of Secondary Education* (1986).

THE QUESTION OF OPTIMUM SCHOOL SIZE

Early analyses of the problem of managing falling school rolls tended to work with assumptions about school size taken from an earlier period: that comprehensive schools needed to be large if they were to offer the range of specialities required by all children across the ability range. Briault and Smith (1980), for example, argued strongly that LEAs should reorganize their schools so as to establish 'the smallest reasonable number of secondary schools and the largest size of schools having in mind distances between schools' (p.245). His argument draws attention to:

> the disadvantages of smallness for a school for pupils to age sixteen: a necessarily more restricted curriculum for the fourth and fifth years; the inevitability of mixed-ability groups; mixed or restricted objective groups for public examinations; greater difficulties in deploying staff in such a way as to use a teacher to the best advantage and yet still ensure that the curriculum is covered. A lower PTR is required, not temporarily ... but permanently to maintain the small school *per se* ... If excellence is the aim ... then the peer learning group must be more than a handful ... I am not arguing that a small school is necessarily a poor school, simply that it has greater difficulties and disadvantages in meeting all the educational needs of all its pupils, which reflect not upon its teachers but which arise simply from its size. (Briault and Smith, 1980, pp.238–9)

This classic argument for a large comprehensive school was in line with that presented by the Secondary Heads Association (SHA) in its booklet *Big is Beautiful* (SHA, 1979). Large, in this context, tended to mean schools with perhaps eight to ten forms of entry.

Professional opinion began to move against very large schools, arguing that such scale was not required to provide an adequate range of curricular experience; in any event, providing only a 'few large schools' would deprive many communities

The challenge

of a school at a time when many were beginning to accept the significance for pupil achievement of close ties between teachers and parents. The argument of minimum size now consented to five or six forms of entry as acceptable educationally:

> Experience suggests ... that 11–16 comprehensive schools of 4-form entry and below find it difficult to offer a curriculum of appropriate range and to provide sufficient teaching groups, without the support of staff: pupil teacher ratios much more generous than the average; such ratios may have to be achieved at the expense of the authority's larger secondary schools. (DES Circular 2/81)

The problem in provision for pupils aged 11–16 is therefore maintaining schools of a sufficient size. Schools below five or six forms of entry find it increasingly difficult to deliver a broad curriculum without staff subsidization. The alternatives are to provide extra staff as rolls fall, to narrow curricular provision, or to close and amalgamate schools in order to keep average school size up.

The greatest problems of contraction often appear at sixth form level. *Better Schools* (DES, 1985) states that:

> A comprehensive school catering for pupils aged 11–16 normally needs to be of a size which enables it to maintain a sixth form of at least 150, if it is to provide an adequate range of A level and other courses. (DES, 1985, p.80)

Some teachers would argue that sixth forms can be effective at a smaller size. Nevertheless, after rising in the late 1970s and early 1980s sixth forms and their teaching group sizes have begun to fall. In 1983, 55.3 per cent of classes had fallen to ten or fewer pupils. The Macfarlane Report *Education for 16–19 Year Olds* (DES, 1980), argued persuasively for the virtues of size:

> We think ... that the size of the 16–19 group must be a primary consideration in the generality of cases. First there is the issue of the range of combination of subjects which can be offered. Attempts to increase that range beyond what the school can naturally support can lead to diversion of

attention and resources from those in the lower school, to their immediate and longer term disadvantage. Next, we think it fair to assume that students are more likely to find stimulus in working together in a group rather than being spread in ones and twos over a number of institutions. Working together in larger groups they are more likely to appreciate the standards and expectations attaching to sixth form study and to draw support from their peers. Finally there is the matter of teaching quality and qualifications; larger groups can more easily justify in the first place and attract (and retain) a sufficient number of teachers of high calibre. We conclude that educational considerations point strongly though not without exception towards the concentration of 16–19 pupils and students into large groups. (DES, 1980, p.28)

The Macfarlane Committee found, as one would expect, that the average group size was higher in sixth form colleges, at 11.6, than in comprehensive sixth forms, at 10.3. The study also found a positive correlation between group size and A level performance. These arguments on size have been reinforced recently by the DES in *Falling Rolls and Size of Schools* (1986) and in DES Circular 3/87, *Providing for Quality*.

RATIONALIZING SCHOOL AND COLLEGE

The process of rationalizing resources to ensure greater effectiveness of educational provision, especially for 16- to 19-year-olds, required the focus to shift beyond the closure or amalgamation of schools to the relationship between schools and further education colleges. Rationalization of provision across the education sectors could eliminate waste and duplication of resources, introduce much needed flexibility in the use of institutions and staff, and most important, facilitate the new objective of developing a vocationally oriented curriculum by breaking down barriers between education and training.

These policy intentions were made clear in a series of consultative documents. In *Providing Educational Opportunities for 16–18 Year Olds* (DES, 1979c) the government expressed concern at the unplanned overlap in provision

The challenge

between the sectors: 'commonly both school and FE sectors are concerned with providing for the 16–18's and often there is overlap between them ... much duplication has undoubtedly occurred because of uncoordinated growth amongst institutions' (p.3). The pressures upon resources and the need to make effective use of plant and teachers, the requirements of students and employers all 'demand flexibility in structures and institutions' and suggest, in particular, that 'it may be necessary to ask whether the present boundaries between school and college are the right ones' (p.6).

LEAs, as Macfarlane proposed, should review the totality of institutional provision in the 16–19 area and consider the scope for extended collaboration between school and college or seek to create new integrated institutions for 16- to 19-year-olds.

The educational as much as the economic argument for rationalizing school and college provision was given significant emphasis. The changing world of employment and the pressing demands of employers suggested a rationalization and redirection of the curriculum for those over 16. Traditional distinctions between training (specific vocational tasks) and education (the general development of knowledge, moral values and understanding) were now outmoded. The rationalization of the curriculum as between school and college would allow 'the well recognized national need for more vocational education of a high standard in the face of major changes in the nature of employment' and enable the country to produce 'the skilled and versatile work-force needed for the future'.

THE RATIONALIZATION OF OPPORTUNITIES

It was well understood, however, that rationalizing provision really presupposed qualitative policy decisions about educational opportunities, that is, about systematizing access to educational routes and thus to the labour market. The rationalization of resources presupposes the rationalization of educational offerings and opportunities. As the treasury official insisted at an Expenditure Steering Group (ESGE) 16–19 subcommittee in 1979, for the members of the committee to determine how to rationalize educational resources they must first address themselves to the issue of *how much* opportunity, choice and access is to be allowed *to which* groups of young people: they must first define desirable levels of participation for the whole age group and then the separate 16–19 'client groups'. The Macfarlane Report incorporated these arguments about the need to rationalize educational opportunities: what was offered in the past may now be unreasonable in cost as well as being unsuited to the nation's needs. The aspirations of young people must be realistic and rationalized from now on: 'that a range of opportunities is available of a quality that meets the realistic aspirations of young people, parents and society at a cost which the nation judges it right to pay' (DES, 1980, p.13). The Macfarlane Committee believed that it was appropriate to define more clearly than hitherto what should count as a reasonable or suitable range of opportunities for 16- to 19-year-olds. Opportunities, they argued, should be seen in relation to the educational and training (or the vocational) needs of different 'client groups'. The committee classified these groups as comprising the different routes taken by young people at age 16: for example, those who enter employment, those who are without work or the prospect of work, those who pursue A level courses, those who seek specifically vocational qualifications in TEC and BEC, or the 'new sixth' who return to education without any clear vocational or educational objective. Distinct groups therefore could be distinguished and differentiated in educational needs and opportunities – 'it is right that young people should branch out at the age of 16, each according to his or her abilities, aptitudes and career intentions' (DES 1980, p.17). Macfarlane was concerned to erase status distinctions between these different vocational routes and thus to promote 'even-handedness of treatments' and 'parity of esteem' between them.

The policy of rationalization of educational provision therefore had a number of dimensions. At the most obvious level it meant reducing surplus capacity in school accommodation and thus promoting the efficient use of resources. This efficiency was taken a stage further, to embrace colleges as well as schools, since the department wished to prevent duplication and waste between school and college. Rationalizing the relationship between school and college, however, was designed more to integrate education and training provision than simply to use resources more efficiently. The economic objectives were a means to achieve educational policy

The challenge

objectives and to improve the relevance of education to the world of work. At this point the more complete rationalisation plan was disclosed. It means a tightening of the relationship between educational 'outputs' and the needs of society and economy through the systematizing of access and opportunity.

The politics of parental choice

Both Labour and Conservative governments, in 1976 to 1980, wanted, especially in a time of resource constraint, to rationalize educational provision but also to make political gains by allowing parents more say in their choice of school. The number of parents who were appealing to the secretary of state over the school they had been allocated by the LEA had increased from about 100 per year before comprehensivization to about a 1,000 a year by the mid-1970s. The Conservative Party was beginning to make this increasing concern the focus of a new strategy of supporting parents' rights in education.

The Labour government of 1976 sought to pre-empt Conservative political advantage and incorporate parental choice within its own policies. Shirley Williams issued a consultative paper entitled *Admission of Children to the School of their Parents' Choice* (DES, 1977). Parents would be given a statutory right to choose a school for their children unless the roll had reached a limit set by the LEA or the authority considered that allocating a place would endanger the comprehensive principle or be at the expense of an efficient use of resources. There was to be a right of appeal, but to an LEA body, with the secretary of state only coming in on procedural matters.

As Tweedie (1986) has commented, these proposals were challenged by a number of people in the Labour Party as likely to undermine the principle of comprehensive education because 'parental choice would distort the distribution of academic ability among the schools'. Yet, 'Though some Labour Party officials opposed parental choice most agreed that parents should be able to choose which school their child attends as long as those choices did not harm education at any schools' (Tweedie 1986, p.5). When the Labour government's 1978 Education Bill entered the House of Commons it was proclaimed as securing choice for parents (H.C. Debate 959).

The Politics of Reorganizing Schools

But as others have rightly commented (Williams, 1980; Stillman, 1986; Tweedie, 1986) the Bill proposed to do more to protect LEAs' duty to implement the comprehensive principle than to establish parents' right to choose schools.

It was, however, the Conservative Party that was from the first more committed to parental choice, which sat more consistently with their beliefs in individual rights. In 1974 the opposition spokesman on education, Norman St John Stevas, announced 'A Charter of Parents' Rights' that was as much a response to the 'black paper' right wing of his party as to the supposed dissatisfaction of parents unable to choose schools. The charter was included in the Conservatives' October 1974 election manifesto:

> A CHARTER OF PARENTS' RIGHTS: An important part of the distinctive Conservative policy on education is to recognize parental rights. A say in how their children are to be brought up is an essential ingredient in the parental role. We will introduce additional rights for parents. First, by amending the 1944 Education Act, we will impose clear obligations on the State and local authorities to take account of the wishes of parents. Second, we will consider establishing a local appeal system for parents dissatisfied with the allotment of schools. (Conservative Party, 1974)

By 1976 the Conservative Party had extended its charter to include parental choice of school. As Tweedie and Stillman point out in their analyses the bases of the Conservative rationale had moved beyond notions of individual freedom and responsibility to tie choice into a theory about the quality of schooling: consumer choice and market forces would reinforce 'good' schools and close those which were failing; choice would lead to greater parental control of education; and, as some Conservatives appreciated, choice would inevitably lead to academic and social selection with oversubscribed schools being able to pick and choose which pupils they wanted to admit. The Conservative manifesto of 1979 reflected the shift in thinking:

> Extending parents' rights and responsibilities, including their right of choice will also help raise standards by giving them greater influence over education. Our parents' charter will

place a clear duty on government and local authorities to take account of parents' wishes when allocating children to schools, with a local appeal system for those dissatisfied. Schools will be required to publish prospectuses giving details of their examination and other results. (Conservative Party, 1979)

The Conservative Party won the 1979 election while being committed to reducing public expenditure – for example by eliminating surplus school capacity – but also to extending parents' rights to choice which, in education, depended upon the existence of some spare capacity.

The dilemmas for local education authorities of reconciling parental choice and efficient provision (of markets and rational plans) became constituted in the enabling legislation: the 1980 Education Act. This act established the principle of parents expressing a preference for a school. The 1988 Education Reform Act completes the revolution of parental choice.

The 1980 Education Act: establishing the principle of parental choice

The enactment in 1980 of the Education (No.2) Bill concluded a two-year period of intensive parliamentary activity in the preparation of four Education Bills by two governments. The purpose of such frenetic activity in Whitehall and Westminster was to prepare legislation that would change a number of the procedures governing education, in order to help local authorities rationalize their provision during a period of contraction but also enable parents to express a choice of school for their children. The Labour government intended to provide parents with an opportunity to express a preference for a school as long as it did not interfere with the LEAs' plans to maintain comprehensive education opportunities for all pupils. To this end LEAs would be granted the power to plan limits to admissions so that some schools would not become oversubscribed at the expense of others. If that happened educational opportunities would collapse in the dwindling schools because staff would be withdrawn and the curriculum necessarily diminish.

The 1980 Education Act articulated the new Conservative

government's perspective on the dilemma of managing contraction and yet enabling parental choice. On a superficial reading, the Act appears to be a rather nondescript collection of disparate items, a miscellany of trifles. Arguably, however, it formed the most important legislation in education since the 1944 Education Act, which established the framework for the government of education after the war. That 1944 act defined relationships between 'partners' to the government of education – ministers, the local education authority, the schools and parents. It divided powers and duties between several partners so that, for example, the Minister for Education would formulate national policy, the local authorities would establish and maintain schools, the curriculum would remain the responsibility of schools, and parents would have the duty to ensure their children attended school. Although the general principle governing the act proposed that 'pupils [were] to be educated in accordance with the wishes of their parents', ostensibly affording them a direct and significant influence in the government of education, the most influential of the partners was the local education authority, and its power grew through the 1950s and 1960s.

The effect of several provisions in the 1980 Education Act was to weaken the authority of the LEA in planning and managing local education. The new secretary of state, Mark Carlisle, did not go as far as some of his party would have wanted, in giving parents the right of unrestricted choice, realizing that LEAs did require some levers to help them manage falling school rolls. Nevertheless, the legislation strengthened the influence of parents.

Whereas Labour had prepared *statutory* 'PALS' (planned admission limits), section 8 of the 1980 Act merely allowed LEAs to publish limits as their planning guidelines, which would enable them to manage local education efficiently. But LEA powers were weakened further in two ways, firstly by parents. Section 6 stated the general presumption that LEAs must comply with parental preferences for schools unless they could demonstrate that admission would prejudice efficient education because of the extra expenditure incurred. The legal adviser to one large LEA argued in a public seminar that according to his interpretation of the law a local authority would find it almost impossible to exclude a child because the authority would not be able to prove that *one* further admission prejudiced efficiency. And each preference had to be taken individually, so that even if there were a whole extra class in the admissions queue each claim had to be taken separately and considered on its own merits. In practice the courts have not taken this interpretation, although the Ombudsman challenged Croydon on these grounds.

The same rules of individual assessment would apply to parents who appealed against the LEA admission decision. Section 7 of the act stated that 'every LEA shall make arrangements for enabling parents to appeal against' the decision of the LEA or, in the case of the voluntary schools, to the governing body. To review such appeals it would be the duty of the LEA to constitute a new 'appeal committee' which would not be chaired by a member of the LEA, although the LEA might maintain a majority on the panel if it so chose. The decision of the committee was binding on the LEA.

In order to help parents make their decision about which school to choose, it would be the duty of the LEA, for each of its schools, to publish information which could inform their choices. It would include not only the admission arrangements but also, by regulation of the secretary of state, would describe the education provided in each school as well as its achievements including examination results. The research of Stillman and Maychell indicates that the number of appeals has grown year by year since 1980, up to 10,000 in 1983: 'In respect of appeals the interpretation of parent's rights is evolving rapidly and the balance between parent's individual wishes and the broader needs of society is still moving toward the parent' (1986, p.188).

The data are more equivocal about trends of actual parental movement in the school market place. The studies of Stillman and Maychell (1986) and that of Ranson, Hannon and Gray (1987) suggest, however, that where LEAs vigorously promote parental choice then parents can pursue and gain the school of their preference. The case study of Manchester in this book will illustrate the growth of market forces in spite of attempts to curb it.

The second way in which the 1980 Education Act weakened the authority of the LEA was by strengthening the power of the secretary of state. Section 15 granted ministers the power to intervene and control admission limits should LEAs wish to change them significantly. Where an LEA intended to reduce the number of pupils in any relevant age group who were to be admitted to the school in any school year to a number which was four-fifths or less of the standard number (1979 intakes), it had to submit to the secretary of state its proposal for his or her approval. As rolls fell from the 1979 figure emerging spare places could allow 'controlled' parental choice, with the secretary of state having strengthened powers to regulate the balance of planning and choice between LEAs and parents. One DES official acknowledged that section 15 was a considerable increase in the powers of the centre (Ranson, 1985).

The 1988 Education Act: completing the revolution of parental choice

The 1980 Education Act established the principle of parental choice, but in an uneasy relationship with the principle of LEAs' planning contraction. Subsequently, LEAs began to plan their provision and to develop reorganization plans so as to respect the principle of choice while seeking to maintain an adequate curriculum and level of staffing for all schools.

For a number of advisory groups linked to the Conservative Party this was not enough (Adam Smith Institute, 1984; Institute of Economic Affairs, 1987; Hillgate Group, 1986). For them, continuing problems of educational standards would only be resolved when the professionals' control over school organization and the curriculum was subordinated to the test of unfettered parental control and choice. The pamphleteers of parental choice argue that parents have an inalienable right to choose the education which their children are to receive. Moreover, an educational system which is accountable and responsive to the choices of individual consumers will improve its standards of performance. As in other forms of market exchange, the products which thrive can only do so because they have the support of the consumers.

These ideas for a radical recasting of the government of education shaped the manifesto of the Conservative Party for the election of June 1987. The manifesto commitments were endorsed in the Education Bill presented to Parliament in November. Introducing the Bill in Parliament, the secretary of state, Mr Kenneth Baker, said:

The challenge

The Bill will galvanize parental involvement in schools. Parents will have more choice. They will have greater variety of schools to choose from. We will create new types of schools. Parents will be far better placed to know what their children are being taught and what they are learning and the Bill will introduce competition into the public provision of education. This competition will introduce a new dynamic into our schools system which will stimulate better standards all round. (DES, 1987c)

Parents are to be brought centre stage in the establishing of an education market place. Parents are accorded choice, influence over governing bodies, and control — if they choose — of new grant-maintained schools. 'Open' enrolment is designed to end the LEAs' capacity to place artificial limits on admission to schools. 'The government is committed to securing wider parental choice within the system of state schools' (DES, 1987a). To this end schools will be allowed to recruit up to their available capacity, defined as physical capacity or 'the standard number' admitted in 1979 (when schools were largely full), or, if it is higher, the number admitted in the year before the legislation takes effect. If a governing body decides to accept a larger number of pupils it can apply to the secretary of state. Moreover, local electors can object to the education secretary if they believe an LEA has set the limit too low.

Parents are to acquire a determining influence over school governing bodies. The 1986 Education (no.2) Act gave parents an equal representation with the LEA on governing bodies. Now the act gives governors responsibilities for school budgets, appointment and dismissal of staff as well as the ability to overrule an LEA on redeployment of staff.

Parents are to be granted the capacity to acquire control of schools if they choose:

> The Government is taking action to increase the autonomy of schools and their responsiveness to parental wishes ... The Government considers that it should ... respond to the numerous indications it has received that groups of parents want responsibility of running their schools as individual institutions. It proposes to provide an additional route to autonomy by introducing legislation ... to enable governors

of county and maintained schools, with the support of parents, to apply to the Secretary of State for maintenance by grant from central government, instead of maintenance by LEAs. The Government believes that this proposal ... will add a new and powerful dimension to the ability of parents to exercise choice within the publicly provided sector of education. The greater diversity of provision which will result should enhance the prospect of improving education standards in all schools. Parents and local communities would have new opportunities to secure the development of their schools in ways appropriate to the needs of their children and in accordance with their wishes, within the legal framework of a national curriculum. (DES, 1987b)

These schools will receive grant directly from the secretary of state and will form a new type of independent school within the maintained sector. Parents will have a determining influence on the governing bodies of newly formed grant-maintained schools.

The 1988 Education Reform Act, therefore, radically strengthens the capacity of parents to exercise choice and influence over local schools (within a strong framework of curricular control by central government).

In this chapter I have described the way central government has responded to the dilemmas of surplus capacity created by falling school rolls. During the 1980s legislative change has gradually strengthened the powers of parents to choose, at the expense of the LEA's ability to provide education securing equal opportunities for all pupils and students for whom they were responsible.

In chapters 3 and 4 I shall examine the response which LEAs made to the pressures exerted by falling rolls. Most LEAs have vivid dramas to recount about their plans to reorganize schools and colleges. It is to these local strategies and politics that the argument now turns.

Chapter 3

LEA strategies for institutional reorganization

Although it was hoped that all LEAs would follow common practice of reviewing and planning change rationally (cf. DES, 1980; 1981) it was nevertheless acknowledged, reluctantly perhaps by some, that there could be no single, national, policy solution:

> Some would say that educational merit, demography and financial constraints point inescapably to the adoption nationally of a break at 16. We think that there are indeed powerful arguments in favour of educating 16- to 19-year-olds in fairly large groups, and are clear that a scatter of small sixth forms offering an inadequate range of options at high cost must wherever possible be avoided. In some areas sixth form or tertiary colleges may be the best solution both educationally and financially. We have considered carefully whether to recommend that education for 16- to 19-year-olds should everywhere be provided in these ways. We do not, however, see that as a practicable policy capable of national implementation, because of the realities of existing investment, and the different demographic prospects of particular local authority areas. We are conscious too of local preferences and the success of many all-through schools, which in some areas may very well exist alongside extensive provision in further education ... No option should be excluded at the outset – what matters is the effectiveness of the chosen pattern. (DES, 1980, p.36)

In the first part of this chapter we discuss the options for

LEAs in reorganizing their schools and proceed in the second part to describe the variety of actual strategies used. In the third part of the chapter we begin the process of identifying the underlying patterns to reorganization.

Institutional options for LEAs

A number of options have been available to LEAs to rationalize their institutional arrangements The alternatives often centre upon whether to retain sixth forms within schools or to separate them out.

RETAINING THE SIXTH FORM

This option proposes that LEAs retain sixth forms within their existing systems of (mainly all-through) schools but ensure economic use of resources and an adequate range of educational opportunities, either by a programme of closure and amalgamation, or by developing 'consortia' of co-operating sixth forms. This system can lead to important advantages to students in terms of continuity and progression in development and in systems of pastoral care. The traditional advantages of sixth form education may also be retained, as young people are exposed to greater intellectual stimulus and academic challenge as well as developing responsibilities for younger pupils lower down the school.

Retaining sixth forms in schools may however have a number of disadvantages: the curriculum may be limited because of the small size of many sixth forms; the stimulus of peers may be lost in small teaching groups; sixth formers may now prefer the more adult atmosphere of college, and many would prefer a fresh start offered by a new institution. Maintaining many small sixth forms is moreover extremely costly, and this is particularly noticeable at a time of contrained budgets.

Consortia arrangements in the absence of amalgamations can help but involve a number of associated problems, as the Macfarlane Report outlined:

> It requires however sustained and positive effort: willing acceptance of the need to adjust timetables, to share specialist facilities and to give up particular courses or

Local strategies

subjects in order to allow them to be provided more effectively elsewhere; close consultation between subject departments pre- and post-16; common policy for example about examination boards or courses to be selected; and sympathy and consistency of style and philosophy. It is doubtful if purely informal arrangements can be satisfactory for long, except to accommodate a particular student or group: a well-thought out policy with arrangements ... is essential. Extra support services may be needed to keep the machinery running smoothly. If the institutions are not geographically close, then time and cost of travel become critical factors; and if students have to move frequently between the two or more institutions they may well lose identity with any one community. (DES, 1980, p.29)

Consortia arrangements were for these reasons perceived by many as the weakest and most unsatisfactory form of institutional system in a period of contraction.

PLANNING 'MUSHROOMS'

This is a hybrid system in which both FE colleges and school sixth forms are retained, but in order to ensure that the size of the sixth form and its teaching group numbers are respectable in the economies of scale they provide, sixth form education is offered in only a small number of 11–18 schools. The remaining schools become 11–16 institutions, whose senior pupils 'feed' into a neighbouring 'mushroom' sixth form. The Macfarlane Report suggested that these arrangements may have been appropriate in the early stages of comprehensive reorganization, because most secondary moderns would not immediately be able to support a sixth form. But the position in a period of contraction is different; they argued that

> Schools which have previously catered for a full range of age and ability may have to adjust to a reduced age range and to seeing their older pupils transfer to other institutions. That still may be the best solution for the pupils, but there are difficulties for the contributory schools. Schools which retain sixth forms tend to have more prestige in the eyes of many parents and are apt to be the most popular first choice for pupils at 11 or 12. The residual schools then suffer both

failing to attract a due proportion of the most able pupils, as well as in limitations of staffing that go with both a smaller school and the absence of advanced work. (DES, 1980, p.30)

Reorganization of institutions according to the mushroom principle could in many ways be seen as a return to the system of schools prior to comprehensivation.

AN INSTITUTIONAL BREAK AT 16

A great deal of educational support from all sides of the 'partnership' was developing for a more radical change in institutional arrangements which would offer, it was claimed, the most extensive range of economic and educational virtues. Many were arguing that the traditional school sixth form not only provided too limited a range of courses for present needs, but, more seriously, was now an outmoded institutional form. As Dean *et al.* (1979) reported, young people, increasingly mature at sixteen, needed a new start, a more adult atmosphere, and more specialist counselling and careers advice than could typically be provided by schools. The benefits of scale and educational advance could be found in the sixth form centre, the sixth form college, or the tertiary college.

The sixth form centre takes 16- to 18-year-old pupils from a number of schools, which may all contribute to teaching at the centre. This arrangement preserves the sense of continuity for both staff and pupils. Concentration of teaching in a small number of centres allows a more efficient use of resources in order to support a broader curriculum. Sixth form centres constituted on this basis, however, may have the same problems as do consortia arrangements: there are timetabling difficulties and it can be more of a struggle to create a consistent ethos if teachers merely travel to a site to teach rather than working day-by-day to establish a coherent learning strategy.

The sixth form college institutionalizes the separation of sixth form teaching from the 11–18 school. These colleges nevertheless are less of a break with traditional practice because they tend to preserve the distinction between academic sixth form work and vocational preparation that would continue to be provided in further education colleges. The college concentrates the virtues of the sixth form while having the advantage of allowing larger teaching groups and a wider choice of subjects, not only at A level but also for the 'new sixth former' seeking a one year extended general education. The college provides a more adult atmosphere that could attract more pupils to stay on in education. In the larger institution better use can be made of teachers in shortage subjects like computing, modern languages and mathematics, while the absence of sixth formers may enhance the status and sense of responsibility of senior pupils in the 11–16 school (cf. Glazier, 1980). For Macfarlane the major claim of the sixth form college is that it 'is an attempt to provide an institution designed specifically and solely for the needs of the full-time 16- to 19-year-old student ... at an important transitional point in [their] studies and personal development'. (DES, 1980)

Counter arguments include the potential unpopularity of such institutions with some staff, who would lose the academic teaching with senior pupils that they have both enjoyed and believed central to their career development. Junior staff may miss the guidance of specialist colleagues who share the teaching of a subject. For many, the most worrying criticism is that focusing on the continued separation of academic and vocational courses and teaching at a time when curriculum development points to their integration (cf. Judge, 1980).

The tertiary college option seeks to integrate in one institution the virtues of academic and practical learning. Ideally, students can choose the mix of courses which suits their particular needs, for example, adding an A level European language to a business studies course. The tertiary college will have a different atmosphere from either school or sixth form college because courses will include adults on a part-time or day release basis (cf. Cotterell and Heley, 1980). Students are typically given more discretion in planning their learning programme. Yet advocates of the tertiary solution recognize the need to develop the qualities of pastoral care that have been the great strength of the sixth form and often too weakly established in the further education college tradition:

> One could say that the prime task of the tertiary college is to unite the caring tradition of the school with the respect for the independence of the individual that has been a feature of the FE college. The young adult needs a more supportive advice system than many FE colleges have developed, but a

less intrusive context than that of the school sixth form. The tertiary colleges have recognised that the key point here is the linkage between the three cornered system of student, pastoral tutor and academic course. (Holt, 1980a)

The argument for integrating the academic and the vocational traditions of postwar provision for 16- to 19-year-olds has a long and eminent tradition but is only now gaining ground (cf. Janes, 1980). Pedley suggested a revised version of the 'county colleges' proposal in the 1944 Education Act, which would provide for this age group as a whole while having regard for the great variety of opportunity needed by individuals within it' (1956, p.165). Mumford called for a 'junior college to provide for all students who wish to continue their education beyond 16 ... Junior colleges therefore satisfy the principles of comprehensive education in a way no other system does' (1970, pp.20–1).

The term 'tertiary college' was first coined by Sir William (now Lord) Alexander in 1969 when Secretary of the Association of Education Committees. Yet although the first tertiary colleges were established in Devon and Lancashire in 1972 there were still only thirteen by 1979. For many (cf. Janes, 1980) tertiary colleges provide the continuation of comprehensive education for 16- to 19-year-olds. For the official group on the Macfarlane Committee they provided the rational solution to the contracting sixth form.

Summarizing the options: most LEAs facing falling rolls will have to review and probably revise their institutional arrangements for the 16 to 19 age group (cf. Packwood and Whitaker, 1988; Challis, Mason and Parkes, 1987). A number of considerations need to be taken into account: assumptions about the pastoral needs of students; the nature of the curriculum (academic and vocational) to be offered; the career needs of teachers; costs; and the effect of post-16 colleges on the remaining 11–16 schools. The politics of education would also intrude.

Those committed to selection would tend to choose the 'mushroom' sixth form; those committed to comprehensive schools but the traditional curriculum would favour the 11–18 school or the sixth form college; while those advocating comprehensiveness in opportunity and curriculum reform would opt for tertiary colleges. Yet just when institutional

Local strategies

options were being debated most fiercely, their importance was thrown open to question by the new curriculum development issue: the learning process rather than organizational structure should become the focus of educational planning. For example, those emphasizing continuity and progression in the curriculum from 14 to 19 introduced a note of caution for reorganization plans that pointed inexorably to the virtues of the post-16 college. For some (cf. Newsom, 1978; Brighouse, 1986; Melling, 1987) this is to institutionalize a division between pre- and post-16 arrangements when curricular thinking points towards a more open, permeable relationship emphasizing continuity in learning.

Variety and struggle in LEA reorganization planning

The conclusions of the Macfarlane Report recognized and encouraged diversity within an emerging trend to post-16 provision. But even those committed to diversity were probably unable to anticipate the enormous variety in policy objectives as well as planning process that would shape strategies of institutional reorganization at LEA level. We shall consider the variety of actual approaches to reorganization planning.

NO INSTITUTIONAL CHANGE: AN EDUCATIONAL OPPORTUNITY

A bold and imaginative LEA such as Coventry (under the leadership of Robert Aitken and Councillor Lister) began by expressing the idealism of educators who perceived falling school rolls as an extraordinary opportunity to develop the quality and comprehensiveness of the learning process. If the authority was to preoccupy itself with institutional questions of closure and amalgamation energy and resources would be directed away from their true target: developing the processes of education. Emerging spare capacity in schools could be harnessed to extend provision for the community, including adult education and the youth and careers services.

Planning for change started in 1981 with the publication of a consultation document called 'The education of 11–19 year olds: dimensions of change' (Coventry LEA, 1981). A working party of elected members was established which took evidence from a wide range of interests. In 1983 a further consultative document was published called 'Comprehensive education for life' (Coventry LEA, 1983). Whereas a great number of LEA planning documents for reorganization are preoccupied with numbers, buildings and contraction, this exciting document is a positive contribution to our understanding about how education should develop through a period of structural change in economy and society. The service should respond to the changing needs of the community and of individuals who would increasingly look to education for support, opportunity and fulfilment in their lives.

The learning experience of young people as well as adults would have to become more appropriate to the times:

> The content of programmes will need to include life, social, personal welfare and learning skills as well as vocational skills and the pursuance of competence and excellence. Direct experience as well as academic learning is required. Students should be accorded as nearly as possible adult status. Such programmes should start before the age of 16 and allow for sequential and progressive development ... for all adults ... the content of programmes, modes of learning, attendance patterns, learning materials and tutorial support systems will all need to be tailored to the needs of adults. Credit systems will need to be developed which allow for interchange between validating systems, levels and institutions and between formal and informal modes. Indirect support from the education service by distance learning and by co-operative input at the work place or home through voluntary community bodies and media is likely to be a developing feature. (Coventry LEA, 1983, p.59–60)

School leavers, increasingly regarded as young adults, would be encouraged to negotiate the learning programmes and be supported by a 'pastoral base' in each community comprehensive school. This base would comprise a devolved careers service, employment officers, and youth workers, as well as teachers in a new partnership of professionals serving the needs of young people and the community.

Given this emphasis upon developing learning for 'life-long education' the essential institutional issue to be grasped was less surplus buildings than the extent to which schools and

Local strategies

colleges actually worked as institutions to support such purposes. The educational leaders of Coventry believed they did not. New educational purposes would require 'fundamental changes of style in learning, in courses, in delivery of programmes, in patterns of attendance, in certification and most important, in the atmosphere or ethos of the institutions' (Coventry LEA, 1983, p.59):

> In contrast to the present system [which] can be likened to a steam railway: you can only progress on the education gravy train if you get on the right train at the right time and with the right tickets. We need to break away from such a rigid delivery system of fixed entry points, of hours in a day, terms, academic years and self-contained levels and entry qualifications. (Coventry Education Committee, 1982, p.46)

In a city already well provided with secondary schools the initial political choice was to retain virtually all its schools as community colleges, and should one or two at the most become 'surplus' they would be converted into further and adult education institutions. Efficiency would be maintained post-16 by setting sixth form group sizes, and encouraging consortia arrangements between schools, with students if necessary using taxis to transport them across the city. We shall need to continue the story of frustrated idealism below.

Another authority to tackle the problem of falling school rolls by focusing upon processes rather than institutional infrastructures, was Northumberland County Council. The Director, Christopher Tipple, proposed an ambitious scheme of 'supported self-study' for those over 16. It was described as

> distance learning technology applied in the school context ... Secondary school pupils will work independently with a multi-resource pack and receive help from peripatetic specialists and other teachers in the school. Three or four periods a week rather than the present eight will be spent with teachers. Development work begins in September 1987, probably focusing on minority A level subjects such as geology and Spanish rather than 'core' subjects such as English. The plan is to produce, over the next five years, materials and resource packs for a range of academic and

vocational subjects . . . In rural areas of the county, therefore, it is expected that this self-help study scheme will enable smaller sixth forms to survive and to offer the same breadth of curricular choice as large sixth forms without the disruption of closures and amalgamations. (Surkes, 1987)

NO INSTITUTIONAL CHANGE: POLITICAL FRUSTRATION

Some LEAs have wanted to rationalize their schools and colleges but have not been able to, being frustrated by the lack of political will or muscle. As the 1980s progressed the chill winds of government cuts in public expenditure forced an authority like Coventry to face the realities of school closure or the consequences of government-imposed financial penalties and even legal challenge in the courts. In 1984 a third consultative document was published, called 'Future choices', which made it clear that school closures were inevitable. A new working party was formed and in 1985 it recommended six amalgamations. There was considerable opposition locally and it required the unprecedented casting vote of the mayor to agree to the closure/amalgamation of only one secondary comprehensive school.

Differences of interest and dispersal of power have worked to frustrate reorganization in a number of other authorities. In Newham in the early 1980s the chief education officer encouraged the members of his education committee to review the extent of surplus capacity in the borough and to initiate public consultation over amalgamations. The ruling policy however was for community education and using spare capacity in schools to extend the participation of adults, youth and pensioner clubs. Pressure was applied by the DES, who gave the authority two months to explain why it had not agreed to a reorganization policy for declining rolls in schools, following a report by the district auditor which claimed that there was urgent need for closures.

Conflict between the local educational interests prevented any reorganization planning in Liverpool, even though the roll fall was one of the most severe in the country, leaving nearly 50 per cent fewer 15-year-olds in schools by the early 1990s. In 1983 the secretary of state put Liverpool under pressure to make proposals for contraction and a reorganization plan was proposed.

Local strategies

The inertia created by divergent interests has affected some county councils as well as urban areas. By late 1986 very little progress had been made on reorganization planning in Hereford and Worcester, and it took an impending crisis in school sixth forms to spur the chairman of the education committee to establish the necessary working parties to review areas of the county and formulate plans. In the Kidderminster and Wychavon areas middle school systems would possibly have given way to 11–16 schools and post-16 colleges, but political divisions emerged over the form the post-16 colleges should take.

PLANNING MUSHROOMS

Conservative controlled Wiltshire county council proposed a 'mushroom' solution to secondary education in Salisbury. Under the plans, the city's two remaining grammar schools and three secondary moderns would have been replaced by three comprehensive schools: two 11–18s and one 11–16 school running alongside each other. The proposals were opposed by a local conservative councillor who chaired the Salisbury schools action group, and by the local Conservative Member of Parliament.

The plans were rejected by the secretary of state, Sir Keith Joseph, because of the academic achievement of the two grammar schools, the number of objectors (a petition signed by more than 12,500 local people) and the capital cost involved (estimated at £2.5 million). The rejection meant that the LEA had to consider alternative plans to meet a projected roll fall of over 20 per cent of secondary pupils by 1990.

REORGANIZING 11–18 SCHOOLS: RATIONALIZING SELECTIVE SYSTEMS

A number of LEAs have planned to amalgamate and reorganize their 11–18 schools. For some, usually county, LEAs this has been perceived as an opportunity to modify their selective systems and to introduce comprehensive elements of the sort introduced by other LEAs a decade or more ago.

In 1986 Devon county council began public consultation in Plymouth, proposing four new comprehensive schools and reducing the eight grammar schools to three. The prospects of receiving approval for the closure of grammar schools were not

The Politics of Reorganizing Schools

encouraging, certainly if experience in Dorset were used as an exemplar.

Here the Conservative LEA and the governing body of a Church of England school proposed closing two single-sex grammar schools, which each admitted less than one form of entry and had a combined sixth form of under ninety, and to merge it with a voluntary controlled secondary modern, creating a new 11–18 comprehensive school. Severe falling rolls would leave, by the early 1990s, total admissions in the town of Sherborne at below four forms of entry, which would rise only much later and slowly to five. The present effect of this fall has been to raise the selection rate to 30 per cent, as compared with 16 per cent in Bournemouth.

The reorganization proposal received the unanimous approval of the working party and the backing of governing bodies, head teachers and many parents. It was, however, opposed by a small but influential 'save our school' campaign. The proposal was rejected by Sir Keith Joseph who was 'not satisfied that given the quality of the exisiting schools, the proposals for Sherborne taken as a whole would be in the best interests of pupils of higher as well as lower ability'. The secretary of state took sixteen months to make his decision.

An even longer-running saga has been the time taken to gain approval for reorganization proposals in Gloucester city. In the autumn of 1986 the LEA received a second rejection of reorganization proposals: this time for 11–16 schools to feed into a sixth form college. The scheme had been rejected by Sir Keith Joseph because it eliminated selective education. He was not convinced that the plan would benefit all pupils, including especially the more able secondary pupils. The authority was left facing a growing crisis of falling rolls in the city which was exacerbated by parents exercising their choice in favour of comprehensive schools outside the city boundaries.

After the second rejection the authority considered asking the Audit Commission to investigate the waste of resources. It also contemplated taking legal advice to test whether the secretary of state was using his powers reasonably. The contraction of rolls was causing considerable distortion of the exisiting educational system as well as difficulties in maintaining the curriculum. The chief education officer, Ron Anderson, commented that 'grammar schools are admitting pupils of barely average ability, comprehensive schools are not fully representative of the whole ability range with a proper balance throughout and are overweighted with pupils of average or below average ability; secondary modern schools are receiving fewer and fewer pupils' (*Education*, 25 April 1986). The LEA now believed that the secretary of state would reject any scheme which did not contain a grammar school component.

Gloucestershire county council proposed a two stage strategy to break the deadlock. A first stage would rationalize the existing system and the second envisaged 11–16 schools feeding a sixth form college. An immediate tactic was to raise the qualifying entry to the grammar schools, thus strengthening the selective principle thoughout the system and also protecting admission to the comprehensive and secondary modern schools. The new secretary of state, Kenneth Baker, responded by threatening the authority with a high court injunction under section 99 of the 1944 Education Act unless it restored the previous entry arrangements for the grammar schools.

In April 1987 Kenneth Baker came to a decision about the whole package of proposals for Gloucester city. He directed the LEA to restore the lower qualifying standard for entry to a boys' grammar school to that obtaining in the previous year but allowed the authority to raise the standard for the city's three other grammar schools. The secretary of state also allowed the LEA to close a fifth grammar school and three secondary moderns, and to upgrade a three/four form entry secondary modern just outside the city to a six form entry comprehensive school. Finally, he rejected the longer term plans to end selection in the city and introduce a sixth form college linked to 11–16 comprehensive schools.

The secretary of state based his direction about admissions on section 15 of the 1980 Education Act which prevents an LEA from reducing a school's intake by more than 20 per cent of its 1979/80 figure without first publishing statutory notices. The LEA, which had previously said that it would not voluntarily restore the qualifying standard agreed, finally, to comply with the secretary of state's direction.

REORGANIZING 11–18 SCHOOLS: A PLATFORM FOR A FUTURE PLAN

In 1977 an ambitious public consultation document, known as the green paper, was published in Haringey. It reviewed the severe contraction of pupil rolls which would soon empty

The Politics of Reorganizing Schools

many of the Borough's schools and proposed options for reorganizing schools, with the preferred option being the creation of a post-16 college. The document courageously identified the schools which would become surplus in each option. It was in many ways a brilliant document, a model of rational analysis but, inevitably perhaps, it caused a political uproar and invited widespread rejection.

In 1980 a second consultation document was published by a new Education Committee chairman and a new chief education officer. This time the paper presented more up-to-date and severe projections of declining rolls, and a trenchant analysis of the implications for the curriculum and staffing of schools. Options were included but no preference was presented in order to allow an open discussion during public consultation. A widespread programme of meetings was organized with schools, governing bodies, teacher associations and community groups. The emerging views often reflected certain interests: thus college lecturers favoured the creation of a tertiary college while the school teachers favoured the retention of 11–18 schools: indeed a strong alliance of left-wing councillors, teacher and community groups argued for the retention of every school as part of the defence of public services against the government cuts.

Although the majority on the education committee may have been in favour of introducing a post-16 college system it decided to retain 11–18 schools, but proposed a programme of four amalgamations that would reduce fourteen schools to ten, including two voluntary aided church schools. This was to retain one more school than the analysis of surplus capacity warranted, and risked parental movement later leading to the need for a further closure. Some of the leading members and officers of the LEA accepted this 11–18 reorganization, seeing it as rationalizing their existing schools but providing the platform for a further proposal before the 1990s to introduce a tertiary college supported by 11–16 schools.

The scheme was opposed by the governing body of a voluntary controlled school but they were not in the end able to prevent the authority proceeding. A more subtle intervention was made by ministers during their deliberation upon the proposal. One minister indicated that the scheme would be more likely to gain approval if the admission limits allowed parental choice. Since 1982, when the scheme was approved, parents began to alter their preferences and by 1986 public consultations had started about the closure of a further school; discussions also began about a post-16 reorganization of sixth forms and the further education colleges.

SIXTH FORM COLLEGES

Although Bolton was the first LEA to have its reorganization plan (for a sixth form college) approved, in 1980, it was the preparations being made in Manchester that were seen by DES officials and by many LEAs as the test case in this period of institutional reorganization. We shall discuss the case of Manchester in detail in the next chapter, but it is useful to have the outlines described here.

This LEA came to establish a number of firm planning principles upon which it would act: it would prepare a development plan for the whole city in order to realize its prime objective of creating a system of schools benefiting all children. It was probable that such a plan would propose a uniform system for the city rather than a 'mixed economy' of different systems in different parts of the city. The authority consulted thoroughly with all the partners to the service: firstly about principles and then about options. The lobbying over the chosen sixth form college system was intense. The secretary of state rejected the authority's proposal, conceding to a well organized parental pressure group declaring that three schools in the constituency of the city's only Conservative MP should remain 11–18.

Sir Keith Joseph did however give reluctant approval to the closure of grammar schools and the opening of a sixth form college in York. The plan meant the disappearance of the 11-plus in 1985, the closure of four grammar schools, and the creation of seven 11–16 comprehensives feeding into a sixth form college. The reorganization meant the removal of 3,700 spare school places. The decision, it seems, involved more than usual anguish for the secretary of state who in the end had to acknowledge the degree of contraction, the degree of local support for the scheme and the low level of objections. If no action had been taken almost 50 per cent of secondary school places would have been empty by 1990. The decision ended a twenty-year saga of proposals and counter proposals in the city.

Competing proposals for change were at the centre of the

The Politics of Reorganizing Schools

politics of reorganization in Birmingham. If Manchester's post-16 college proposal was conceived by DES officials as providing the model for a 1980s reorganization, then the outcome of the Birmingham case provided the model for ministers.

The city faced a high roll fall, and was particularly disadvantaged in having a large number of small secondary schools, which would become expensive as rolls fell. There was an early statement by officers to elected members that 'there is a need for positive forward planning for the city as a whole'.

In late 1977 the chief education officer had been asked to review the future of 16–19 education. An interim report (Birmingham LEA, 1977) was produced in March 1979. Work on reorganization continued within the LEA throughout 1979 and 1980, with officers facing a pressing need to take action but members being unwilling to face the political opposition that was inevitable. Finally, as in Manchester, a development plan for the whole of Birmingham was prepared for public consultation with a paper which outlined facts and options. A two month period was allowed for consultation. The two basic choices identified were the introduction of new institutional arrangements at 16, and a system based on 11–18 schools. A mixed system, said the consultation paper, had been agreed by an all-party working group of councillors, to be 'a most unsuitable development'. The responses to the consultation document illustrate the range of interests and values involved. As the CEO's February report said:

> Amongst parents, the majority seemed to express a view either for a break at 16 or 11–19 schools. Opinion was evenly divided on these two alternatives. About half of those favouring 11–19 schools were expressing support for a limited range of specific schools.

Specific interests dominated the general. The unions came up with a range of responses. The only common factor in the responses overall was the argument that decisions should be made on educational and not financial grounds.

The report of the CEO, John Crawford, encouraged the members to adopt a rational, system-wide view, reminding them that 'they are taking decisions regarding the whole system upon which the service will operate for the city as a whole for the remainder of the century'. (Birmingham LEA, 1977)

Local strategies

The authority adopted a comprehensive solution, involving a break at 16, the establishment of tertiary colleges and the cessation of the authority's maintenance of the grammar schools that remained within the system. The Birmingham proposals were submitted to the secretary of state in autumn 1981, before there had been a response to Manchester's submission. There was heavy opposition to the plan from those who wished to maintain the grammar schools. It is unlikely that the plan would have been accepted in any case, given the emergence of the 'schools of proven worth' criterion. But the threat to the grammar schools made this rejection certain.

The need for a decision from the secretary of state was pre-empted by the local elections in May 1982, which brought a Conservative administration to power in Birmingham. It seems likely that the decision had been delayed in the hope that it would become unnecessary. Certainly the DES civil servants had been requesting large amounts of further detailed information from the city's education department. On the night of their election victory the city Conservatives sent a telegram to the DES withdrawing the plan. The incoming administration acknowledged the need for reorganization and set about producing its own plan. But it did not feel that any substantial consultation was necessary given that the Labour plan had involved extensive consultation. It produced a revised plan, by June, based on four principles:

1. Falling rolls remain a serious problem in the secondary school sector. The proposals must include the removal of a large number of secondary school places.
2. There are successful school-based sixth forms in a number of schools and these should be retained, but other forms of 16+ education would be considered.
3. The proposal should make provision for some single sex schools to be retained.
4. The grammar schools have an important part to play in secondary education in the city and this should continue.

A plan proposing a number of school closures and amalgamations, and a mixture of 11–16 and 11–18 schools and sixth form colleges was produced. It was rapidly submitted to and approved by the secretary of state.

The proposal that was finally implemented was a mixed

economy, allowing parents to choose within a diversity of provision. The city was also left with an amount of overprovision of places as the Conservative administration was unwilling, in the face of political pressure, to close as many schools as it originally planned. There were a number of smaller schools and it was clear that some of these would close in the future. The Conservative plan implied that this would happen by 'market forces', as parents opted for certain schools, leaving the less attractive schools to close. This Conservative implemented reorganization was based on incremental adaptation rather than rational planning and global principled action.

Since the Conservative plan was accepted and implemented a number of schools have indeed been closed. In 1984 the local Labour Party regained control of the city and still faced the issue of rapidly falling rolls and high youth unemployment. A tertiary solution is still favoured by the group but has not yet been proposed as part of a formal consultation exercise. In large part this is because the authority is reluctant to go through the whole debilitating political process again, or face the unpredictability of the decision by the secretary of state.

The effect of the rejection of Manchester's proposal together with the delays and withdrawal of the Birmingham schemes was to discourage others and to slow down the impetus to prepare reorganization proposals. It was only by 1985 that some major cities such as Sheffield and Leeds began to nerve themselves for the political struggles involved in city-wide tertiary college proposals.

THE TERTIARY COLLEGE SOLUTION

A number of LEAs have proposed schemes of reorganization involving the integration of further education colleges with traditional academic sixth forms to create new tertiary colleges; these would provide a comprehensive range of courses in education, training and vocational preparation. Some proposals have been accepted by the Secretary of State. Sir Keith Joseph approved a tertiary college and three sixth form colleges for Croydon after a previous proposal had been turned down for being too novel. Although Croydon took legal advice they did modify their proposal in the end, and it was accepted by ministers because it protected the curriculum and it ensured that young people were differentiated.

Local strategies

More recently Kenneth Baker as secretary of state has approved schemes of tertiary reorganization in South Tyneside, Stockport and Sunderland, indicating a more flexible policy towards the tertiary solution. Other LEAs have been less fortunate and tertiary proposals prepared for Durham and Swansea have been rejected, while there has been considerable delay in approving Dudley's proposal to turn sixth form and FE colleges into a tertiary college. Nottinghamshire has shelved proposals for tertiary level because it believes it is unlikely that it will succeed in the present climate. Shropshire, however, is proceeding with its intention to create a new tertiary college at Bridgnorth.

A number of big cities have been preparing major schemes of tertiary reorganization, including Leeds, Liverpool, and Manchester. They are reflecting anxiously upon the fate of Sheffield's proposal as well as upon the uncertainty of the current political climate.

The politics of the Sheffield reorganization in many ways replicated the saga in Manchester that will be discussed in more detail in the next chapter. Sheffield proposed to reorganize its 57 middle schools and 36 comprehensive schools into 37 12–16 schools feeding 7 new tertiary colleges. These proposals were opposed by the Alliance and Conservative Parties and, in particular, by 'an articulate body of middle-class parents' in the more affluent south-west corner of the city. The Association of Sheffield Parents opposed the lack of parental and pupil choice at 16; the eliminating of sixth forms of proven worth; and the unrealistic costings. The secretary of state turned down the scheme in November 1986 and informally agreed that six schools in the south-west of the city (all in the constituency of the only Conservative MP in the city) should be withdrawn from the scheme and retain their sixth forms. Six rather than seven tertiary colleges would be created.

Labour members of the Education Committee in Sheffield were said to be pleased that they had achieved so much, and believed that the support for the remaining 11–18 schools would wither in time. The authority's plan was to be implemented from September 1988.

The Politics of Reorganizing Schools

Identifying the patterns of change

In spite of the obvious variety and apparent inconsistency in national decision-making about reorganization proposals it is possible to identify trends since the late 1970s. At national level both Labour and Conservative governments, as well as the DES, have acknowledged that a national policy for rationalizing institutional provision should allow LEAs the flexibility to accommodate diverse local circumstances. Nevertheless, governments have formed views about which institutional strategy would best implement their own policies of rationalizing resources, curricula and educational opportunities.

Two general strategies have dominated central government policy on institutional reorganization since the mid 1970s. Common to each has been a certain view about the relationship between institutions, the curriculum and 'good' education:

COMMON INSTITUTION AND DIFFERENTIATED CURRICULUM

The preferred policy option amongst professionals and governments from the late 1970s until 1982 was the establishment of post-16 colleges fed by 11–16 schools. These colleges were regarded as more economic in their use of resources, and at the same time as widening the educational opportunities for young people. In sixth form colleges a range of A level studies could be provided that was beyond even a large traditional sixth form, while resources allowed the development of prevocational courses. The post-16 college came to be regarded, in conventional wisdom, as the way institutions should cater for an increasingly distinctive age group.

This strategy was the preferred solution of the dominant faction within the DES, of the Labour administration under Mrs Shirley Williams in 1976–9 and of the Conservative administration under Mr Mark Carlisle. For the Left, post-16 and especially tertiary colleges were the comprehensive spearhead into the 1980s politics of reorganization. For the Right, such colleges were efficient in their use of scarce resources and allowed the development of a more vocational bias and the differentiation of students according to ability and aptitude.

The argument for the common institution and the differentiated curriculum was given expression in the DES:

Local strategies

[There] will be increasing differentiation of routes at 16, the academic A level route will become more intensively academic and a jolly good thing too. Within each track there will be different but intensive provision. There will be some switching of courses – about as much as there was between the secondary moderns and the grammar schools. (senior DES official, cf. Ranson, 1985, p.63)

Mark Carlisle published the report of the Macfarlane Committee which developed this DES argument. It encouraged the view that post-16 colleges would be the best solution educationally and financially for many LEAs as well as arguing that young people should become more differentiated at 16, although there would be 'parity of esteem' between the different curriculum tracks.

Local and national planners had the same objective although investing in it alternative interpretations. In Manchester, Leeds and Sheffield the LEAs perceived post-16 colleges as extending the comprehensive revolution of expanded educational opportunity. At the same time central planners saw them as rationalizing efficient provision and allowing differentiation in educational achievement.

DIFFERENTIATED INSTITUTIONS AND CURRICULA FOR CONSUMER CHOICE

This strategy followed from a particular understanding of institutions. Institutions create a distinctive ethos that will shape students' experience and achievement and therefore, if different educational outcomes are sought, this will best be accomplished in different institutions which can concentrate on different purposes. If post-16 colleges develop a more vocational emphasis, as some hoped they would, then the quality of academic courses might be threatened. The sixth form, it is believed, is indeed the nursery of academic virtues, for the lower school as much as for older pupils, and needs therefore to be retained – in some schools. The implementation of this policy would encourage the retention of grammar schools, the acceptance of reorganization proposals which favoured the 'mushroom' 11–16, 11–18 solution, or closures and amalgamations which ensured efficient use of resources while protecting institutional diversity.

These arguments gained the support of two of the four education ministers during the Macfarlane Committee's existence and were responsible for the moderation of its tertiary recommendations. The second Conservative administration under Sir Keith Joseph (1981) comprised, arguably, the victorious remnant of the previous ministerial team: that is, those ministers who were committed to schools rather than colleges, to the virtues of the grammar school and the traditional sixth form, and to giving parents as much scope as possible to choose between the different institutions, believing that the quality of schooling is much improved if made responsive to consumer preferences.

The scale and quality of a school's sixth form was made a defining characteristic of the 'worth' of a school and a key principle in planning reorganizations. Thus Circular 4/82 said:

> The secretary of state regards it as essential that when local education authorities consider the educational and financial factors they should bear prominently in mind the need to retain what is best and has proved its worth within their existing system of secondary education. He will not normally approve proposals which have as their consequence the closure or significant change of character of schools which, by demonstrating their success in the provision they make for sixth form education have already proved their worth under existing arrangements and in his judgement can continue to do so.

The implication of the commitment to consumer preferences together with the policy on sixth forms favoured a mixed rather than a uniform strategy on institutional reorganization. That is, parents should be given the opportunity of sending their children to schools as well as colleges, and to schools different in kind. As rationalization proposals have been submitted to the secretary of state for approval his judgements have reflected, wherever possible, the values of maximizing parental choice and institutional diversity, including the protection of selective grammar schools. These values and principles of central government have been used to override the values and decisions of local authorities, except in the unusual circumstances of a consensus forming within an area in favour of a particular option. This explains the decision in York but also in Manchester, where the secretary of state intervened to break up the LEA's plan and to accept a proposal which

Local strategies

allowed sixth forms as well as colleges. If Manchester's original 'scheme' exemplified the aspirations of the earlier model for reorganization, then Birmingham's final plan could be seen as providing the canonical form of institutional diversity for those LEAs still in the planning process.

Reorganization planning in limbo

The thin pattern of reorganization planning had by early 1988 entered a period of uncertainty, though the likely outcome is a strengthening of the principles established by Sir Keith Joseph and continued by Kenneth Baker. The general election of May 1987 allowed the Conservative Party to put into practice its manifesto promise to prepare legislation to transform the government of education, radically extending the principles of consumer power initiated by the 1980 Education Act and extended by Sir Keith Joseph. The 1988 Education Reform Act will leave the LEA bereft of many of its powers.

In this context a number of LEAs have decided that pursuing the difficult process of planning reorganizations and of gaining political support for them, is now futile. Sutton, Warwickshire and Nottinghamshire have all during the autumn of 1987 shelved their proposals to reorganize schools and await the outcome of the new legislation. A number of LEAs will consider that the radical extension of the market in education probably means the end of much reorganization planning: some schemes may well encourage some of the affected schools to 'opt out':

> Local Education Authorities are increasingly getting the message that only piecemeal reorganization schemes will get approval. But this will only increase the delays and add to the administrative burdens on both central and local government. (*Education*, 11 December 1987)

Indeed, during August 1988, after the enactment of the Reform Bill, the secretary of state suspended consideration of school reorganization and closure proposals so that schools threatened with section 12 or 13 notices could consider opting out and prepare submissions for grant-maintained status.

Thus national and local politics are inextricably interwoven in reorganization planning. It is to a detailed account of the politics of reorganization planning that I now turn to, in the case study of Manchester LEA.

Chapter 4

Reorganizing schools in Manchester: a case study

A case study has the advantage of providing a more detailed understanding of the processes of change in education. The story of reorganizing schools and colleges in Manchester illustrates many of the general issues we have to consider: the balance of planning and choice, supporting the curriculum and the teachers, consulting parents and the community, the changing relations between central and local government, and the opposition of organized interest groups to LEA decision-making. The disadvantage of a case study is its uniqueness, its lack of representativeness. Yet there is little doubt that, in the eyes of many senior figures in central and local government of the period, Manchester's reorganization was to be an exemplar to other LEAs. There has indeed been a lot to learn, and the experience of other LEAs suggests that the case of Manchester is not after all unique; it reflects the experience of many counties as well as metropolitan districts.

The background

Manchester's scheme for comprehensive reorganization was approved by the secretary of state in 1965 and implemented in 1967. It had been planned locally with the support of the Labour government: 'Crosland needed some LEAs to show comprehensive reorganization could be done. We were given generous capital funding to facilitate reorganization: we called it "the sweetener"' (an officer).

The Politics of Reorganizing Schools

Nevertheless, in spite of such generosity, no purpose built comprehensive schools were established: 'the best are those created by additions and modifications to schools originally built in part to a different brief' (senior education officer (SEO)). This period of partnership between central and local government, as well as cross-party consensus, was illustrated in Manchester when the Conservatives won power in the city in 1967 and the new Chair of Education honoured the implementation of Labour's reorganization plan.

Although from the outset there had been concern about the potential size of sixth forms in some of the new schools, both parties decided to retain the system of 11–18 comprehensives, even though in 1970 the Conservatives had considered a sixth form college in the south of the City. Sixth form performance, however, became an issue in the 1970s, as 'black papers' of this period began to challenge exam achievement in Manchester. While professional analysis of exams produced a more balanced picture of performance the LEA became increasingly aware that, with small uneconomic sixth forms, the institutional conditions did not exist in Manchester for effective educational achievement for 16- to 19-year-olds.

By 1976 other factors reinforced the concern. Officers increasingly appreciated the severity of the impending fall in school rolls. The number of children born in Manchester in 1962 was 13,600. In 1978 it was only 5,660. In 1958 there were 115,800 pupils in Manchester schools, yet in 1978 there were 97,000 and in 1986 it was projected there would be only 67,000. That contraction could imply as many as 70 surplus forms of entry in county and Church of England schools, and mean reducing 26 11–18 schools to 10 or 12. The issues for planning were well known: as well as poor participation and performance post-16, there was the financial constraint of pressure from central government to cut expenditure and a 'surplus' of 800 teachers; a weak Church of England sector which nevertheless wanted its own sixth form; a significant Muslim community wanting single-sex education for its girls; and inner city deprivation and decline matched with parental preferences for moving their children out of the inner city. Given these constraints, one thing at least was certain: 'doing nothing' was not an option.

Manchester

Preparing for change

The LEA perceived an opportunity amidst the constraints 'to improve the performance and efficiency of the education service'. The chief education officer (CEO) was quite clear about the principles required to approach contraction. (His own account of the reorganization process can be read in Fiske, 1982). At the North of England conference in 1979, he counselled his colleagues to 'tackle the problems with vision and boldness [because] the opportunities for creative results far transcend the difficulties'. The vision required the ability to prepare a development plan for the next five to ten years, but also to 'lead positively towards an open and a public debate' that would seize the challenge of improving standards and quality in secondary education.

To protect and enhance the educational opportunities for all children, the LEA formed the belief that the only option was 'to plan the education system as a system'. Not only did this mean, at secondary level, choosing one system – whether it be 11–18 or 11–16 and post-16 colleges, and avoiding at any price a 'mixed economy' – it also meant re-examining the whole system, primary and post-primary. Improving participation and performance for 16- to 19-year-olds – 'which is the key to our decision-making' – meant reviewing the whole spectrum of provision, beginning with the primary end:

> Our strategy is to go at the whole thing serially, stage by stage, taking the decision on 16–19 in the context of falling rolls. The first stage in the plan is to link secondary high schools with a number of 'feeder' primaries. This will allow us to sort out primary rolls which enables us to calculate secondary rolls. The second stage of the plan is to tackle 16–19 in this context. 16–19 will fall into our lap once we have created a dynamic between primary and secondary. (senior education officer)

The underlying assumption in planning was that there is a necessary relationship between the quality of education experienced by young people and the institutional arrangements provided: the curriculum offered, the range and quality of teachers, the resources and books, depend upon the size of classes and the LEA being able to predict with some certainty the numbers on roll. The capacity to predict the size of 11–16 schools, and beyond that more concentrated sixth form numbers depended upon the capacity to control the 11-plus transfer. Feeder primaries would facilitate planning of numbers and provision but also significantly allow stronger links between school and community, which the LEA was increasingly perceiving as vital to the quality of learning.

This desire to plan the system as a whole meant they had to challenge one of the principles which had existed since reorganization in 1967: the right of parents to choose their comprehensive school. By the mid 1970s this sytem of parental choice was beginning to fail: parents' choices were not being met, there were appeals and growing dissatisfaction. The chief education officer's analysis was more stringent: at a conference at York University in 1977 he argued that parental choice was 'ruining Manchester's comprehensive schools'. Forceful and articulate parents used pressure to ensure their children entered favoured schools. This was distorting the social and intellectual balance of school intakes. A hierarchy of school popularity with parents had been established 'appearing to include elements of tradition, fashion and prejudice'. The chief education officer added: 'Whatever it may be called the result is certainly not a system of broadly similar comprehensive schools. Some argue that it is not a comprehensive system at all'. Parental choice, market forces and the social selection which followed was, it was proposed, undermining the provision and therefore the opportunities of many children, especially in inner city Manchester.

In September 1978 the education committee approved the feeder primary scheme. Parents still retained the right to choose a place in another school if places were available. Evaluating the scheme in 1982, the CEO commented 'to date the educational benefits of the linked system and in particular the bridges in the curriculum that it has been possible to build between primary and secondary schools totally justify the change'.

Proposals for reorganizing 11–19 schools

Manchester's development plan moved into its second phase in July 1979 with a report to committee on falling numbers and secondary school provision: 'this was the starting gun' as one senior officer put it. The report set out the stages of decision-making: to consider the forecasts, options, and particular schools. There would be consultation at each stage. The autumn of 1979 was devoted to wide-ranging consultations on the first stage. A report in October 1979 gave forecast of secondary pupil numbers between 1980 and 1991; the accommodation capacity of existing premises; the range of alternative institutional arrangements; and the number and suggested size of secondary schools required in the 1980s. An extensive round of consultations was arranged, with eight public meetings, as well as discussions with the teachers and, for the first time, with the party groups. Comments and observations were invited and many submissions and petitions received. We shall discuss the significance of the public in decision-making below (in the following section).

The CEO set out the principal questions facing the reorganization exercise in an address to the teachers in November 1979: should the LEA

i) plan or proceed piecemeal;
ii) develop a uniform or a mixed system;
iii) preserve the 11–18 system;
iv) decide upon a different pattern of post-16 education?

The LEA sought reaction to these questions in an open public debate, although with an anxious eye on the need for urgent action.

At the centre, therefore, of the LEA's deliberation at this stage was the question whether one system of provision should be chosen for the city as a whole or whether different kinds of provision could sit side by side. The preference of the LEA was unequivocal:

> However hard you look at Manchester, to break it up into different areas for different kinds of provision, you cannot in fact do it. It is so difficult as to be virtually impossible ... In any case there is a deeply held view in the Education Committee and indeed in the education service that the service in Manchester is a whole and that a uniform pattern is to be preferred. (CEO's address to Manchester's teachers, 6 November, 1979)

The Politics of Reorganizing Schools

The belief in an integrated scheme was to inform Manchester's planning and proposals: a mixed system could only 'lead to first and second class schools'.

In April 1980 the education committee received a report on the public consultations and asked officers to prepare for July a report which set out a series of detailed options (three schemes for 11–18 and four for 11–16, plus colleges). The city council decided then (in July) that from 1982 there should be a break in school provision for all young people at the age of 16, and the education committee was asked to consider the detailed plans in October before further consultation. Two options were prepared: scheme A was based on the principle of scale, that an effective school required eight forms of entry, and defined seventeen new schools; scheme B was based on the principle of relating the schools to the local communities and defined twenty schools. Each scheme described three sixth form colleges, which were to be linked closely to the colleges of further education in an integrated tertiary system. The move to full tertiary colleges was considered an option for future development in the 1980s. Schemes A and B were put out for public consultation in the autumn of 1980.

The politics of choice and consultation

Any educational issue typically involves a great diversity of interests, which decision-making has to strive to reconcile. In this reorganization the interests were potentially highly fragmented, and the views articulated were very intense and assertive. The teachers, the Church of England, the parents and the community groups all had to be taken into account. Even a unified view within the ruling Labour Party could not necessarily be taken for granted, as Left and Right began to fracture, creating a context of great uncertainty for the decision-making process. We shall review the emerging perspectives in turn.

THE POLITICAL PARTIES

The lead and impetus in the reorganization planning had come from senior officers. But any reorganization of this kind would inevitably become political and require strong political leadership. For a time that seemed to be lacking amidst the divisions within the ruling group: some began by retaining their commitment to 11–18 schools, while the majority, including the increasingly powerful Left caucus, preferred to introduce tertiary colleges as the comprehensive solution to falling rolls.

An experienced Chair of Education had been elected to Parliament in 1979 and then replaced by a less experienced and energetic man. During the uncertainty of the local election in May 1980, the chief education officer set out to develop political support for an overall plan. In June he met the leader of the council, who had also the experience of carrying through the 1965–7 comprehensive reorganization. The leader asked for the chief education officer's recommendation; the chief education officer insisted first upon hearing a political view: 'I want to know how tough a report to publish and I got the reply to publish as tough as I liked'. (The effect of this was indicated by an officer: 'There was a distinct change in the CEO from April to July [1980] and the difference was the strong political support he had managed to win from the leader. In July he got the formal decision for a break at 16.')

The leader, previously a supporter of all-through comprehensives, had re-assessed comprehensive achievement and become a champion of tertiary colleges as the comprehensive solution to falling rolls. His stance had the effect of securing a political alliance between the centre-Right and the emerging Left caucus of the Labour Party. He persuaded the education caucus at a crucial Sunday morning meeting early in 1980:

> I told the meeting we must define our objectives and not stumble into the issue. I said that the real socialist policy for 16 to 19 is tertiary colleges because they offered a full range of curriculum, open to all, and suited to need. Tertiary extended the comprehensive principle to post-16 education. I thought we would have an uphill struggle but only two demurred. There was agreement that tertiary colleges extended comprehensive education. (Leader, Labour group, 1980)

This was a decisive moment in party decision-making which had begun with a policy conference of the party the previous year and an inconclusive working party on falling rolls.

The Politics of Reorganizing Schools

The Chair of Education also had come around in his thinking to accepting the importance of tertiary:

> I had preferred 11–18 schools but it was not working well. Bright youngsters were leaving to get jobs and the unmotivated were leaving often for the dole. Only the middle band were staying on but the sixth form provision was too academic, unsuited to many who needed a broader curriculum. A break at 16 was now right but which option? Sixth form colleges in my opinion are still academic which suggests the tertiary solution ... What we cannot have is a mixed system: we must be able to provide educational choice and opportunities to all children in the City. (Chair of Education, March 1980)

The decision filtered through to officers:

> The Labour group has decided the 11–18 system had not delivered the education they wanted. It has not delivered the A levels, nor the comprehensiveness – and they will look for a comprehensive reorganization as a political decision which will divert criticism and channel support. The group had indicated that they have decided upon tertiary colleges. They have consulted. They want to receive a report before the election (in May 1980), they will deliberate and decide after the election. (education officer, March, 1980)

The politicians' dilemma, however, is that a decision which is sound educationally may not necessarily be popular electorally:

> The Labour members are losing support fast by talking about school closures. The fine tuning of policy is done at the street corner. It depends on whether an election is imminent. We will have a decision on 16–19 after the election. In the end the decision in Manchester will be a political one. (an officer)

The Labour group also had to consider the need to gain approval from the secretary of state and acknowledge that tertiary colleges might have to be the final stage of a development which would take a number of years:

A tertiary system of sixth form colleges and FE colleges is a watering down. I went along with it because politically we stood a better chance of approval from a Conservative government and because time is important: we needed to reduce buildings and expenditure. (Leader of the Labour group)

Meanwhile the Conservative opposition, even though in 1970 it had considered sixth form colleges as appropriate for Manchester, was becoming firmly committed to 11–18 schools. The leader of the Conservatives on the education committee perceived a proposal of sixth form colleges as merely a stage in the longer term development of tertiary colleges and that this should be opposed on political as well as educational grounds:

> Although sixth form colleges (school colleges) have been successful in smaller towns tertiary colleges have not. The Tory Party nationally has not accepted tertiary and locally we are totally opposed. If Manchester gets tertiary colleges then the country will go tertiary.
> The arguments against tertiary are (i) that we have first class FE colleges with specialized training linked up to the Training Boards; (ii) these massive comprehensive colleges will destroy the influence of the academic sixth form while fudging successful FE work; and (iii) the colleges will draw the best teaching staff away from schools
> I oppose these colleges as a Tory. They can be used for political ends. We have 20 Marxist councillors and we battle in May to see whether we will have a Marxist council. They will use education for social planning.
> Some of these issues were fought in the national Macfarlane Committee. The Prime Minister is not prepared for tertiary education at this stage. There is a fear in the Tory Party of social engineering, of the further comprehensivization of 16–19 education leading to the comprehensivization of the universities. (Leader of Conservatives on the education committee)

The local Conservative MP for Manchester Wythington articulated another element of Conservative Party philosophy: its commitment to the principle of parental choice of school, and the idea that linking primaries to secondaries would be destroying parental rights; and just to oppose Labour: 'parental choice is the public expression of consumer satisfaction and local authorities should recognise it as such' (*Guardian*, 21 November 1978).

Whereas the local Conservative Party retained allegiance to national policy, the local Liberal Party diverged. Nationally, Liberals were proposing a tertiary solution to falling rolls, but the party in Manchester was influenced by local pressures to retain some 11–18 schools and so proposed a mixed system of schools:

> The problem in Manchester is the problem of the inner city where we have not produced a good education service. De facto, 11–16 schools have been developing in the inner city while successful 11–18 schools have been growing in the suburbs. De facto, a mushroom system had been developing.
>
> We propose spending time on the inner city schools and making them work first, and upon making the inner city sixth form college show the way to the south of the city.
>
> The other strategy for education in the inner city is to get housing and the environment right in order to restore social balance in the intake to schools. The Liberal Party has been pushing for less municipalized housing: the middle class have been driven out of the inner city and so have the skilled working class. The only way to get education right is to get housing right. (Liberal councillor)

There were differences amongst senior professionals as much as amongst councillors.

THE OFFICERS

The officers in Crown Square were no less divided than other participants in the Manchester story. Some began by supporting the 11–18 system while others were committed to the idea of a break at 16 and introducing sixth form colleges. One senior officer from the outset was a passionate advocate of tertiary colleges. The CEO would not express a preference in the early stages: 'he is completely enigmatic: his managerial style is that he is the last one to choose' (senior officer). 'I **think** he is for a break at 16: but he does not have a line; he is the least doctrinaire person I know' (deputy).

Manchester

But the alliances within the office formed and changed over time. The majority of senior officers became committed to sixth form colleges while the deputy came to lead the tertiary cause. It was, said one officer, the CEO who first began to use the language of a tertiary 'system', and this integrated the interests within the office. The general shift within the office to a post-16 college solution followed educational as well as political influences:

> We all brought different approaches ... What started the planning was the demographic problem of numbers and the problem of A levels. But although we started off in the direction of a number-crunching exercise within a narrow educational issue, we changed direction. Why? The talking and talking, and reading [Holt, 1980a] on the tertiary system so that we came to look at the educational needs more broadly as well as the system requirements.
> We have gone through an educative process. We knew we could not stand still. We have learned. The members too have taught us: local government officers are like butlers, they respond to their employer's view. They have taught us. I went in early on and reported that the members had to start with the people (teachers) they had, to protect the ethos of the institution, the top end of the market. I was taken apart by the leader: he told me that the system must be properly tertiary. The system must look after the totality of needs of 16- to 19-year-olds. (deputy)

What began for many officers as an issue of numbers and surplus capacity became an issue of developing the curriculum and purpose of learning. The traditional post-16 (sixth form) education dominated by academic A level 'subjects' stood for a limited learning process and fixed conceptions about learning capacity. A broader, more appropriate curriculum would encourage wider access to education, argued a senior inspector. Thus the thinking about institutional arrangements came under the influence of a richer educational philosophy.

THE TEACHERS

The heads and teachers were a significant interest group in the politics of Manchester's reorganization:

The Politics of Reorganizing Schools

> The CEO had chosen to launch his report in 1979 with the teachers – with his professional colleagues. They are *the* important group. The teachers must be with you. We have a long committee tradition of listening to the teachers. The CEO spoke strongly and was well received. It was clear from the questions how the lobbies would line up. The Wythenshaw gang would line up against closing 11–18 schools. (an officer)

The teachers were divided. The Manchester Teachers Association (MTA) branch of the NUT was, early in 1980, probably about 45 per cent for a break at 16: some teachers were worried about losing out to the FE sector in any new tertiary colleges based upon FE regulations.

The CEO chose to make another strategic intervention, following his talk with the leader, with the headteachers:

> My meeting with heads was as important as that with the leader. They came to see me in July 1980. It was time for a 'Grand Seigneur' performance. They said I should have consulted them. I said we had. But they felt we should not have moved until we had their support. I came down very hard. I said I occupied a statutory position and it was my right to take a view. They had gone too far. This strong presentation worked with the middle ground of undecided heads. The south Manchester opposition, of course, went out screaming.
>
> I have been very interested recently in the number of heads who are now making public statements in support of our scheme as being the only educationally sound scheme although against their immediate interests. (CEO)

A recent President of MTA had done a lot of lobbying. He saw that the 11–18 scheme was only defensible in one part of the city, and therefore it was unreasonable to offer different opportunities to different parts of the city. The majority of heads (Secondary Heads Association) came to accept this argument and to support a single system based upon post-16 colleges.

The teachers, too, had begun to shift their ground. Crucial votes which had been lost were now being won:

Manchester

The mass of teachers began to swing away from the 11–18 model because it implied huge schools in the inner city, although many of the Left in the MTA were still for 11–18. It took an extra meeting of the MTA to get the break accepted: the vote changed not so much because people changed their minds but because more of the moderates were mobilized to come and vote. The left included the Poundswick teachers' lobby which believed that six forms of entry (fe) would provide a viable 11–18 school. (an inspector)

The NUT were committed to a uniform system and to 11–18 schools. But the problem of providing uniform 11–18 schools persuaded many in the end to shift their position. The inner city schools would be penalized because of the need for massive amalgamations leading to split site schools. (General Secretary, MTA)

The National Association of Schoolmasters/Union of Women Teachers (NAS/UWT) had teachers in the Roman Catholic schools (which had moved in 1977 to sixth form colleges) and in the FE colleges. The NUT had a large proportion of primary teachers and women teachers who were supportive.

Material factors also counted. The teachers' jobs and conditions were protected while the decision to favour, in the first instance, sixth form colleges, secured the teachers' A level interests against the impending threat of the FE sector. 'The teachers have been bought on the basis that these are traditional sixth form colleges and that the jobs will go to the teachers' (officer).

THE MUSLIM COMMUNITY

The Muslim community, in Manchester as much as in other parts of the country, made a vociferous case for an all-girls school, in this case in the Longsite and Rusholm area of the city at Levenshulme:

Levenshulme is a successful multi-cultural school. It is very well supported by the Muslims. They wanted Levenshulme as an all-girls school. A campaign gathered – they are very strong – and the committee made it very public that it was conceding to the Muslim group. The knock-on effect of that decision has been considerable. (Inspector)

The creation of a single sex girls' school created an imbalance:

> The case for a single-sex school in the inner city is not good: all education should be mixed-sex provision. I would have gone for an imbalance of provision (having provided for the Muslim girls), 900 now, with a bulge in the primaries. We had a responsibility to put up a co-educational scheme, which we did to test the water — which was very hot. We need therefore two girls' schools, not two boys'. I would have lived with that imbalance. (senior inspector)

The repercussions of the decision to have a girls' school at Levenshulme were felt in negotiations with the inner city and with the Church.

THE BLACK AND WORKING-CLASS COMMUNITY

The inner city community — Afro-Caribbean and white working-class — began late to organize a campaign in support of two schools for Moss Side, to save Ducie as well as Birley. The committee took a decision to keep open Ducie, but as a single-sex boys' school to balance Levenshulme girls':

> Ducie is a hostage to fortune, an unintended consequence of the Muslim community's desire for a school for girls. Ducie is good enough to keep. It has problems but it does a good job. Moss Side does have a need for two schools and Ducie has the support of the community. But Ducie is now the weakest part of the plan. If anything does not survive that will not. (senior inspector)

The authority was also facing a strong lobby from teachers and parents in East Manchester. The protest complained that the plan did not offer enough secondary schools.

> There were not enough numbers to justify a six form entry (fe) school. So we reintroduced Nicholls Ardwick (extended by St Gregory's which we negotiated with the RC sector)

and we relocated the High School of Art which had a strong lobby supporting its retention and in a new home. We had originally planned to locate the High School in the vacant Ducie site but of course now had to think again. Locating the school in the east of the city enabled us to offer two fe local needs and 4 fe for city-wide intake. (officer)

The High School had been a small school with a distinctive ethos supporting the arts and a pleasant social mix. Considerable (middle-class) pressure ensured its survival in the reorganization plan.

THE CHURCH OF ENGLAND

A further repercussion of the Levenshulme decision was on the Church. Church of England schools in the city were, as in many other parts of the country, 'voluntary controlled': that is ownership remains with the Church but the schools are maintained financially by the LEA. Voluntary controlled schools are effectively controlled by their LEAs, nevertheless, the LEA cannot ignore their interests. Change requires careful negotiation.

In Manchester the original proposal from the Church of England was that they be granted two 11–16 schools and a sixth form college to meet their needs (their existing provision included two small schools). The LEA countered by offering one school and no college. The authority was prepared to look for improved premises to house an integrated 11–16 school for the Church:

> The CEO is bargaining with the Church of England. He is offering them buildings and an interest-free loan. (an officer)

> The problem with the Church of England is that they have had two very different governing bodies: Fallowfield has two fe and is equivalent to a middle-class girls' grammar school. Openshaw is more like a working-class secondary modern. It is not easy to get an arrangement between them about a joint school. We had agreed that they should have Levenshulme Upper but that got lost with the Muslim bargaining. (inspector)

The LEA then offered Levenshulme Lower and Fallowfield High which would have needed a building programme. But the Church of England began to negotiate with the RC church for the St Iquatious schools (six fe, near to the university in the city):

> The Church is considering taking these schools with a devious view to keeping Fallowfield and using it as a sixth form college in the longer term. If they get St Iquatious in the centre it will kill Ducie stone dead. Ducie is over the road. It would have a knock-on effect, leeching city centre kids from Ducie and from Birley. The Church's commitment really is to the girls' grammar school rather than to a church school. This Church of England situation is just a different means of introducing selection. (officer)

The LEA was torn – between a belief that the more appropriate role for a Church school was in the inner city playing a missionary contribution and the knowledge that that part of the city was already over-provided with schools and that it needed to control intakes.

CREEM AND THE CAMPAIGN FOR 11–18 SCHOOLS

Each of the interest groups we have considered could be accommodated, sometimes with difficulty, within the LEA's proposals. But the 'campaign for the retention of eleven to eighteen schools in Manchester' (CREEM) challenged the very principles behind the authority's proposals. Because retaining 11–18 schools almost certainly involved more closure and either a mushroom or a mixed system, it meant that CREEM was challenging the idea of planning the system as a whole. And, by fighting for some schools, CREEM challenged the assumption that the whole was more than the sum of its parts and that all should contribute to the changes necessary.

Yet frequently it is the case that parents do not want *their* school to close. Especially if it appears, or indeed is, a successful school. The campaign had its roots in the well-to-do south of the city, which supported schools with large sixth forms. It began when the Head of Parrs Wood School in Didsbury called a meeting of his Parent–Teachers' Association in October 1979 to inform them of the LEA's original consultative paper on reorganization. A vote was taken then which aimed to retain the school in its existing form and to invite parents of other schools – primarily in the south of the city – to attend a meeting in order to get themselves organized in time for the LEA's consultative programme in November. After that meeting a number of schools began to organize themselves. Interestingly, those that did organize had strong PTAs or Parent Associations and, crucially, a head committed to action.

Although the Parrs Wood campaign had middle-class support, it was the action organized around the more traditional working-class Poundswick School which led to the creation of CREEM and which provided the dynamic for the parental campaign. The first meeting of CREEM was held in February 1980, with sixty parents attending. A committee was formed, chaired by a cab driver, and including a university professor and lecturer, a biochemist and a bank manager. Public meetings were arranged and petitions circulated. The committee and its chair were particularly skilful in publicizing the campaign, in the *Manchester Evening News*, on Radio Piccadilly, through leaflets and booklets. Funds had to be raised to support the campaign through concerts, dances, jumble sales and charity evenings (cf. Carey, Forum V.12/2; 1981)

CREEM began to organize itself politically. Although intending to be non-political, the leadership of the movement consisted of the leader of the Conservative group on the Education Committee, the Head of Poundswick and the chairman of CREEM. The Conservative councillor began to organize deputations. The first, in September 1980, was to Baroness Young, Minister of State for schools. CREEM believed it received a sympathetic hearing although the minister had, properly, not communicated any opinion. A press statement was published.

In September 1980 CREEM published its booklet on *The 11–18 Solution*, which included mushroom schools in part of the north of the city. They claimed, by the end of the consultation period in the autumn of 1980, to have 50,000 signatures in favour of retaining 11–18 schools.

SUMMARIZING THE CONSULTATION

By Christmas 1980 the authority was completing its second

phase of extensive formal consultation since the issue of reorganization had become a public debate in July 1979, seventeen months previously. The CEO had become concerned that the consultation should enable particular interests to be expressed but that the responsibility of articulating the needs of all children should remain with the LEA:

> It is coming over strongly from the public consultation that parents are not interested in discussing the whole system, the problem of establishing efficiency etc. They are only interested in where their child will go.
> Social class is never far below the surface in public meetings and negotiations. Although it is the middle-class interests which are vociferous in the south and north around the two old grammar schools. There is a great silence in the centre of the city; the working-class interests are quiet. It is the officers who are articulating a system which will protect their interests. Although the ethnic voice is to be heard against CREEM, against creating one system for whites and another for blacks. (CEO)

A report to committee on 12 December 1980 summarized the autumn consultation. There had been eight public meetings together with a variety of other consultations with parent-teacher groups, school teaching staff, the Church, area consultative committees, the teacher associations and governing bodies of the FE colleges. The several views were made available to committee in a large appendix. The report summarized them as:

> In large measure the views of individual parents reflect particular concern about changes in linked primary schools, about the provision to be made for single-sex (girls) education. There also remains a measure of organized support for the retention of sixth form provision in certain schools currently running sixth forms of 100 pupils or more. The expression of this view is strictly speaking outside the November consultations, but is relevant to the extent that it challenges the principle of a break approved by the City Council in July.

It also reported that there was a balance of opinion in favour of scheme B in the north, central and Wythenshaw areas and a marked preference for scheme A (larger schools) in the south area. A preference for scheme B was expressed by the main teacher asssociations.

The report proposed to make extra provision available for girls and to retain Ducie. These changes would do much to reduce, though not entirely eliminate, parental concern over primary links proposed in scheme B, the local pressure for retaining larger schools in the south, and a concern for two single-sex girls' schools. It was recommended finally, in January 1981, that approval be given to nineteen new county and one Church of England aided secondary schools, and three sixth form colleges for 1 September 1982. Authorization was given to the issue of statutory public notices of these proposals, in accordance with section 12–13 of the 1980 Education Act.

Public notices of a scheme or proposals?

Section 12 of this act requires LEAs, if proposing to reorganize their schools, to publish their proposals. If there are objections and if the secretary of state chooses to see them, the LEA is required to submit the proposals and the objections together with their comments: 'The DES have told us that they want all the objections, not only the statutory ones' (an officer). (A statutory objection was one made by 'any 10 or more local government electors for the area'.)

The officers in Manchester were keeping in very close touch with the DES at all levels, territorial officers as well as junior and senior officials. It was the first in a new series of reorganizations and a learning experience for both sides: both wanted to get it right:

> The DES looked at our exercise very favourably – it had been a very open exercise. We have kept them fully informed at every stage with all our committee papers and consultations. They have therefore all the information they could want. The statutory objections will not produce anything new for them. (an officer)

A meeting was arranged with (mostly junior) DES officials to discuss the form of the public notice; it was told that it had 'got it

90 per cent right, but improvements could be made.' It encouraged Manchester not to publish annual admissions for 1982–86 and only to publish the 1985 levels, assuming that admissions would not have been above that level until 1995:

> We wanted to plan for a 15-year period and avoid a further reorganization or publication of notices. So the DES advised us to pitch our school sizes in the Notice at a point where further contraction would not exceed the 20 per cent limit set by section 15. The DES were happy to approve this.
>
> The system we are designing leaves very little slack for parental choice. The committee has agreed and the DES seems happy. The DES were very helpful. They told us not to publish all the detail – you would be creating problems for yourself. The only thing we were cagy about was that the Act requires you to publish your transitional arrangements. But we were nowhere near knowing that. We will have to evade that with a generalized statement. The DES seemed happy with that too. (an officer)

The central issue in the Notice, however, was whether it should describe a series of separate 'proposals' for each school, or a unified 'scheme' of interdependent schools. This concern was related to the authority's anxiety about the powers of the secretary of state 'to modify' an LEA's proposals. Could the way the Notice was drafted limit or even prevent ministerial intervention, it was being asked:

> Modification: this is a nice one about which we have not heard the last. I've primed the CEO: section 12/6 of the 1980 Education Act and circular 2/80 para 8/3 says that the secretary of state is not empowered to change the scheme, only to modify by deferring or changing the size of a school. I tackled a DES official about it – what are the precedents? He said there are none. 'Is it just a flyer?' I said. He agreed.
>
> So we drafted our notice as *one* proposal. Not in the plural of a number of separate schools. This is geared to the proviso that the secretary of state can change the scheme only marginally. In our scheme, now, one change could significantly, radically, change our overall scheme. So what it offers the public is one scheme, singular. But the DES are replying by using the word proposals: they are keeping their

options open! That could be a worrying sign for us. (officer)

The CEO met the authority's solicitor to discuss the issue of 'modification': when is a modification a major change; when does administrative unreasonableness obtain? The education officers in Manchester came to believe, following this and other legal advice, that the secretary of state would not be able radically to change their scheme.

In February 1980 the secretary of state formally called in Manchester's proposals, giving them a month to submit their comments on the nineteen statutory objections.

The battle for the minds of ministers and the department

The pattern of planning comprehensive reorganization in the 1960s was based upon close liaison between central and local government, in which agreement was sought before the stage of public consultation. The CEO's strategic planning reflected this understanding of the recent past. Strategy centred upon persuading officials, inspectors and ministers in Whitehall of the validity of the authority's scheme:

> The connections with the centre are vital. We have friends. I meet an HMI in Hale library, my deputy is on the Macfarlane Committee, I will talk to one of the deputy secretaries and I will see the secretary of state. In the last resort I will visit the back door of his home (my standing would enable such access). I hope to get a more formal hearing. My strategy is to recommend an audience for CREEM with Carlisle so that he hears the partiality of their case and so that it provides a precedent for an audience for ourselves at a crucial later stage. (CEO)

The CEO spent a lot of time with the DES. He was increasingly concerned about the growing uncertainty:

> The DES are very secretive at the moment. I have probed how long it will take and get different answers from different levels of the office. We have got a feeling of uncertainty. You have to go up and down the Branch to get information. But

The Politics of Reorganizing Schools

they did at least know about our proposal. In this instance there had been continuity of staffing. (CEO)

The Manchester officers did not believe that the DES had a grip on the proposals coming into Elizabeth House, although it was acknowledged that Manchester was the model for those following to learn from. A new under secretary agreed that the DES had to speed up. The CEO sought more clarification from the secretary of state and arranged to see him privately:

> The secretary of state has told me that educationally it is straightforward. But the problem is political. He is under great pressure to do something other than agree to Manchester's scheme. But the lawyer in him says that he must have sound reasons, he must have justification for interfering (although he does not need reasons for agreeing to the scheme).
>
> What is causing us a lot of anxiety is the politics of winning ministerial support. We are now in danger of being schizophrenic – designing a scheme to get secretary of state approval and one that we can operate educationally. The DES at Minister of State level are not interested in tertiary links, nor on limits to institutional independence. Our view is that we must look to the needs of the whole age group. The ministers are not interested in this. This is the political reality we are facing. (CEO)

> One minister of state came up for dinner and we talked. S/he argued that we must hang on to the sixth forms to feed the universities. I was asked whether the 11–16s would be staffed with teachers who could deal with the high flyers, what could be done for the 15-year-old high flyers – should they take assisted places. The government realized there is little mileage in saving the remainder of the grammar schools, therefore they will free individuals to use the independent sector; offer the public information on academic standards at A level. (CEO)

The response of the authority to the growing uncertainty was to organize seminars at the DES for officials and HMI to make presentations of the proposal, to ensure detailed understanding of the case:

HMI were more up to date about the local issues than DES officials. They knew about the interest groups, the arguments and the lobbies. We felt with them, especially the local inspectors, that we did not need to argue the case for a break, only what kind of institutions they would be. Our local HMI was for a sixth form college. He was worried that the tertiary system might not really develop: it will need strong central planning – planning at institutional level would lead to a free-for-all. I agreed that the whole thing could be a disaster if we could not produce and provide good administrative arrangements, adequate course needs and adequate student numbers. It will need very strong control of courses. We must rationalize courses and be in a position to tell post-16 consortia you can provide this course and not that, you can only accept this number etc. We are still thinking it through. (senior inspector)

Senior officers and inspectors in Manchester, interpreting the emerging messages from ministers, DES and HMI, appreciated the need to cool ardent supporters of tertiary level at home:

My task is to hold off the advocates of tertiary in the office as well as the left-wing councillors. Arguing for tertiary at this stage would bolt the minister of state, and underestimates the willingness of NUT to stay with us. (CEO)

Officers were trying to hold together the fragile alliance of interests supporting the proposals. But the campaign of CREEM to build their own alliance continued. CREEM had an audience with the secretary of state in March 1981. Its deputation included representatives of nine schools, and both Conservative and Liberal councillors. When the Liberal councillors presented the case for a mixed system CREEM was asked whether it would accept such a compromise. The chairman of CREEM accepted it as a possibility (Hargreaves, 1982). (The leader of the Conservative education group had by this stage modified his view and accepted the idea of one sixth form college in the centre of the city).

Local papers commenting upon this meeting gave conflicting reports; one was that the secretary of state would refuse permission to Manchester to reorganize schools: one report spoke of 2 schools, another 5 and another 10. This prompted the local authority to take legal advice:

> The chief executive has written to the secretary of state asking him to confirm, deny, or clarify these reports. We feel we have him game set and match because any rough confirmation would prejudice his position legally. Indeed, he has already prejudiced his position. We are prepared to take out an injunction in the High Courts. (CEO)

In the summer, when the authority believed that a decision was imminent (Fiske, 1982), a Cabinet reshuffle saw Sir Keith Joseph and Rhodes Boyson replace (the demoted) Carlisle and (the promoted) Baroness Young. CREEM believed this new team would favour its cause (Hargreaves, 1982).

Locally, officers perceived the political situation as becoming more uncertain, with the possibility of a 'hung' council following the 1983 local elections: 'if the secretary of state delays a decision the local political context could allow our plan to be unpicked' (CEO).

A new alliance with the Conservative MP for Wythington in South Manchester strengthened the influence of CREEM in Whitehall. Hargreaves (1982) describes Mr Silvester as 'the busy linkman' between London and Manchester, constantly telephoning, writing letters, meeting people. The chairman of CREEM met the minister of state in Blackpool at the Conservative Party Conference (Hargreaves, 1982):

> The latest news is that they were disposed to reject our scheme. Read the *Telegraph* on Saturday. The protesters (CREEM) were going off to the Conservative Conference in Blackpool to celebrate their success. We have news that the minister passed through Manchester *en route* to Blackpool and had lunch with our Conservative councillor.
>
> Last Thursday there was a big ministerial get together in the DES. The minister went to that meeting having been in cahoots with the councillor and confident of getting a rejection. We knew that the meeting may have gone in our favour.
>
> We have got the message from civil servants and HMI that we would not hear for two weeks and that there would be no decision until after the party conference. They asked us

more questions about our submission – who had turned the tide? The civil servants and HMI *and* the lawyers: their advice is that a rejection is not on, that if it went to the courts the secretary of state would lose, as overriding his powers under S.68. (CEO)

The final bargaining

Communication between London and Manchester intensified: 'there has been frantic phoning going on'. DES officials were telephoning the Manchester education office and asking for more information on curriculum support for the 11–16 schools, on A level statistics and on the transition for staffing: 'We were asked for the revenue savings and "told" that separate provision for Muslim girls post-16 must be changed to separate provision for all girls. We feel that the DES are looking for a means of criticising us' (junior officer).

Meanwhile, on the political side telephone calls from London sought more information from CREEM (Hargreaves, 1982): views of Liberal and SDP wanting a mixed system were noted, as were the views of the ethnic minorities wanting an all girls school. CREEM believed political pressure was paying off.

The adversaries of central and local government took recourse to law to gain judgement about their scope for discretion. Both the DES and Manchester had taken legal advice on 'modification' and on the length of time the secretary of state could take to make a decision:

> The DES is now under two constraints: firstly, the time they can take. I got a mandamus during the summer, getting legal advice on how long would be reasonable for the DES to consider our proposal. I got the answer 'nine months'. Secondly, the extent to which they can modify. The legal advice to both the DES and to ourselves was that to extract two or three schools from our scheme would not be a modification but a new scheme.
>
> There has been a consensus of advice. We know, because the legal people like to put their heads together to see whether they have come to the same judgement. We also know the gossip in chambers had been that Carlisle had been desperately wanting to intervene to modify our scheme

(to prevent Boyson and Young rejecting it) but had been informed that the modification clause in the 1980 Act prevented him. We may be saved by *that* Act! (CEO)

The ministers were getting boxed in. A senior DES official phoned the CEO and asked whether the scheme could be delivered for 1987 and asked that Manchester not issue a writ against the secretary of state in the next two weeks (because of the delay).

> I told him that I would hold fire but that I had booked a meeting with our QC in chambers for the 7 November. The hawks in the council want to take them to court. The boys at the top of the DES have been slow in getting on top of this one. They did not get on to it until August. It has been slowly going up the office. They could fudge Macfarlane but they can't fudge our scheme, they have to take a decision. If we get a flat no, there can be no action for another three years. (CEO)

The LEA and the secretary of state: an opportunity for bargaining?

Activity heightened before the decision: 'there was a period of dramatic phone calls from the DES asking for more information to support the proposal'. Just before the secretary of state made his decision he summoned the LEA to a meeting:

> The DES have been taken by surprise by the secretary of state, who had his own mind and was not prepared to be shifted by them. We were summoned to a meeting with the secretary of state and I took the chairman.
> He told us that he was minded to reject but he was giving us the opportunity to persuade him not to. It was a funny meeting. There was no permanent or deputy secretary and no HMI, and there was no conversation, rather a series of questions and answers.
> He said he had a statutory duty to protect the parents' rights and interests. He accepted our financial and administrative arguments and complimented the chairman on following Circular 2/81. But he did not find any merit in the

notion of uniformity. He was interested that the teachers were for that, but parents were against. He said that the parents were more important than the teachers.

The secretary of state said that he could not modify the proposal and exclude three schools because he would be vulnerable legally though if he had the powers he *would* exclude those schools. (CEO)

It appeared to the Manchester delegation that the secretary of state was opening up the possibility of negotiation even though he acknowledged that he was not empowered to negotiate:

It would have been interesting if we'd said OK to his excluding schools if that's what he wanted. (Some of us had considered reorganizing in stages.) But we would then have been in a position of having to persuade local members and teachers: the committee would have been vulnerable; the chair would have been vulnerable to his party — he would have been torn limb from limb.

But it was undoubtedly a moment when we could have played different cards. As it was we told the secretary of state we were not giving an inch. The uniform scheme was the basis on which the consensus locally had been built. (CEO)

The situation required flexibility, but the actors at the bargaining table had their hands tied by the law and the fragility of their respective political alliances. It was also the first occasion in a new round of reorganizations nationally: the actors involved did not realize that bargaining was appropriate behaviour at this stage. The rules of the game were being developed as the game unfolded. Another officer described the sense of constraint experienced by the LEA 'negotiators' but also the emerging differences of principle:

We only got support because of the principle of uniformity. It was the basis of the consensus. Not one teacher association objected. That was extraordinary. We got agreement on the basis of proposing equitable arrangements for all schools losing kids. All schools should take their fair share of contraction.

The Politics of Reorganizing Schools

> The critical thing in our scheme is the taking out of spare capacity. It is very tight, perhaps too tight! There is no spare capacity – but only safety nets (for example, 7 forms of entry in an 8 forms of entry building). This would enable us to say to a parent 'this is your school unless someone drops out of another school'. Spare capacity could cause the collapse of our education system. The secretary of state commends our reduction of capacity but he wants choice as well. (senior officer)

The issue had become, for the the principal adherents, a conflict between planning for the general interest and protecting the rights of individual parents:

> The issue, so Joseph argues, is about big government, bureaucracy, corporate government and ordinary people. He argues that we are trying to impose, enforce, our system on unwilling parents. We are denying individual rights. He is siding with the parents against the bureaucrats and corporate government. (senior officer).

The decision

On the 13 November 1981 an HMI arrived at Crown Square with three letters: for the CEO, the Chair of Education and the Chief Executive, from the secretary of state, rejecting Manchester's proposal:

> [The] secretary of state is now satisfied that on balance the potential educational advantages which the authorities claim for the majority ... are not sufficiently certain to justify the damage which will be done to some schools which have proved their worth under existing arrangements. He believes that only in very exceptional circumstances can it be right to reduce the age range from 11–18 to 11–16 of secondary schools of proven quality which continue to demonstrate their success in the provision they make for sixth form education. The secretary of state does not accept the change proposed by the authority in the organization of such schools can be justified merely because it secures a uniform pattern within the authority. He is particularly concerned

that the proposal would have on Burnage, Parrs Wood and Whalley Range High Schools ...

He shares the city council's belief that an early rationalization of their secondary schools is urgently needed on 'educational and financial grounds' and 'he looked to the city council' to proceed to a reconsideration of their proposals and to publish and submit to him revised proposals which take account of the reasons for his decision at the earliest practicable date.

The letter was regarded in the Manchester office as 'clever': it was technically a rejection and not a modification. Yet the wording hinted that a modified submission could be acceptable to the secretary of state. It was clever in that the letter would not justify Manchester taking the secretary of state to court.

Reflecting on what was to be done

The unity within the Manchester Education Office began to fray a little after the rejection of the proposal. A group of senior officers met to consider how the LEA should respond to the decision, a situation which now included an election in May, together with the increasing urgency of falling rolls coupled with parental choices.

The officers agreed that the only way to proceed, surprisingly, was to accept the modification implied in the secretary of state's letter: that is, to propose the original scheme with the exception of the three schools and go for immediate implementation in September 1982. Another group, including the chief education officer, continued to argue for the principle of uniformity, opting for closure of the weak schools and delayed implementation, in September 1983. But the argument against this position was persuasive and gathered support:

> There is a crisis now: 5,500 16-plus kids are in a system of collapsing opportunities. We must act for them. The short term expedients don't solve the issue: in fact they are such nasty palliatives that they would kill off sixth form provision in most schools. It would cripple school sixth forms. These proposals are negative: implementing section 15 closures and limiting intakes, etc, still leaves us with fifteen forms of

entry surplus, especially in the centre of the city. This strategy would fill up schools in the north and south of the city and empty schools in the middle. That strategy would come close to implementing the CREEM policy and leave half the city bare of schools. We argued that schools offer more than a single (academic) objective – they are community institutions as well. (officer)

The local inspectors supported this analysis. A senior inspector believed that the short term measures would lead to mushroom sixth forms and, implicitly, the return of selection: 'it would take us back to 1966'. The chief inspector's analysis made the case for action especially imperative:

At first I was for a delay, but I came to a different view having looked at the consequences: the implications of delay are worse than the rush for 1982. Both are undesirable but the delay would be particularly disadvantageous. What are they – falling rolls? We could not reduce intakes sufficiently to stave off the collapse of the inner city schools. They would fall to four and three forms of entry and require extraordinary high staffing to protect their curriculum. Such wealthy staffing would bleed even the bigger schools because their staff would have to be reduced to 'pay' for the staffing of the smaller schools.

The notion of delaying was understandable. It is an emotional period. But I believe the problems are so great we have to act. If you examine the detail there is no alternative.

The scheme has to propose the most effective/efficient use of teacher staffing. Our scheme was the soundest educationally that could be had. The money you spent on staffing numbers was the most effective in terms of balance of staff in schools and the curriculum offered across all schools. The diseconomies of staffing would be critical if nothing were done. (chief inspector)

The search began for a political alliance to support the implementation of the modified scheme in September 1982. The chairman, at first, was shocked at the proposal but came to accept it as the only solution, given the need to act urgently to protect the inner city schools. As one officer said, 'Once you do the mental somersault – of accepting modification – then

September 1982 is possible.' A journalist and city councillor were canvassed to influence other members. The education group (Labour members of the education committee) met on a Sunday, listened to the CEO and the chairman and voted for modification and 1982. One councillor said 'Without action there will be no sixth form provision in the north west of the city; we want a sixth form college.' Lobbying began to ensure a majority at education committee and in council: 'people were counting votes calculating that they might just be able to carry it.' 'The chair was saying we don't want any more consultation; we don't want any more lawyers' (officer).

The Liberals and SDP members began to associate themselves with the plan and with the Labour group. The teachers were more distressed, having based their commitment on the principle of uniformity and became divided. The heads chose to support Secondary Heads Association (SHA) and Manchester Head Teachers Association (MHTA) as did NAS/UWT acknowledging the need to act now in the interests of the pupils. The Education Committee carried the proposals on 30 November 1981.

The LEA wanted to organize a meeting with the secretary of state to consider future proposals but he refused:

> It would not be right for me to do so because of my quasi-judicial role in deciding on further proposals made under S.12 of the 1980 Education Act. Statutory objectors might have grounds for complaint if there was any evidence that any new proposals had been agreed in advance between the authority and myself. (secretary of state's letter to Manchester councillor)

Discussion began with the DES about whether consultation was necessary and about the form the notice should take. The DES accepted the argument that there was no need for further consultation because what was being proposed was only a modified form of the original scheme. They also accepted the LEA's argument for publishing one integrated proposal. The officers were implacable:

> We say that uniformity once more is an essential feature of the new proposal. If anything it is more integrated. Educationally, socially, politically we should not agree to

exclude any more schools. The secretary of state has strengthened our resolve to have a single notice because he could pick off more schools now. (A school in the north is now asking to be excluded.) It is as Leibnitz said: we are in a situation of contingent necessities: all the bits of the scheme hang together: they depend upon each other. (officer)

A further proposal, delegations and a decision

In February 1982 the authority made a further proposal to reorganize its schools and create sixth form colleges, with the exception of the three 11–18 schools named by the secretary of state. The emphasis was upon the implications of further delay and the urgency of immediate action:

> The accelerating fall in the number of children transferring from primary to secondary schools each year has now reached the stage at which no county high school receives a full intake by dependence upon its feeder links alone. All schools have some margin of spare capacity – in some cases very large ... and this means that increasing numbers of parents are now exercising their freedom to claim places at schools other than those designated.
>
> The effect in September 1981 was to produce a very uneven distribution of pupils between schools, with ten achieving 90 per cent or more of their admission capacity. A further five schools took between 75 and 90 per cent of their capacity. Seven schools admitted only half or less – in some cases considerably less – of their capacity ...
>
> [A] contributory factor to the decline of these schools has been the attraction of an increasing spare capacity in schools outside the inner area ... The city council's first concern must be the continued health of their county high school system to provide an effective education for all ... The evidence of the preceding paragraphs is that the excess of capacity already apparent in the majority of schools, allied to a heavy skew of parental choice to schools in the outer areas, has seriously undermined the ability of as many as six inner area schools to guarantee a viable comprehensive curriculum to the pupils already on roll. The difficulties will be further exacerbated by reduced intakes in September

1982 when as many as twelve of the existing schools may well attract fewer than six forms of entry.

> To defer a plan for reconstruction beyond September 1982 ... is to invite the collapse of a large part of the Manchester secondary schools system. (paras 26–32)

The LEA believed that the secretary of state had given the authority the necessary signals that he would accept the modified scheme; his letter pointed to such an outcome and so did his statement in Parliament, that is, that if Manchester were to resubmit for 1982 he would welcome it and give it urgent consideration.

The main opposition to the proposal, as before, came from the alliance of parents, teachers and the Conservative Party known as CREEM. They met the secretary of state and officials at the DES on 1 February 1982 and objected to the lack of consultations about proposals which implied that there were not other schools of 'proven worth' in Manchester. CREEM offered an alternative 'mushroom' proposal of nine 11–19 schools and eight 11–16 schools together with one sixth form college, which would widen parental choice. In March the Minister of State for Education received seven deputations of councillors, parents and MPs of which some were in support of the proposals and some against. On the 11 March 1982, having considered thirty-five statutory objections, the secretary of state gave his approval to Manchester's scheme of reorganization.

A continuing saga

The mixed system began to be implemented. Particular emphasis was given to the development of a coherent tertiary system with the establishing of area boards to plan the staffing and courses of the new sixth form colleges and the existing Further Education colleges. But the obvious flaw in the system – over-provision in the south of the city – was soon to become apparent, bringing with it the need for repairs and further plans for reorganization. A senior inspector anticipated the problems in 1981:

> The key problem from my point of view lies in the south of

the city: the southern college. Look at the geography of the south together with the exclusion of the three schools. A large swathe of the city will have to be included to support that college. There is no doubt that the college in the south will now take a long time to get started.

This links for me with a most significant issue. There is no doubt in my mind that the independent schools have organised to try and defeat the sixth form colleges, especially in the south where they have Manchester Grammar School, Wythenshaw High School and another one in Fallowfield. They feared a successful sixth form college would undermine the independent schools: there would be a better, a more extensive curriculum, facilities, library, capitation etc. And parents could send their kids to such a college for free! Just think of our proposed 800-student sixth form college with 400 in a year group. Just think of the staffing that it can provide, the curriculum it could offer, and we hoped to spend £50,000 on the library – it would have been better than the Central Library! (senior inspector)

In the event the sixth form college began to decline. In 1985 the CEO commented that Arden College was not able to live with the competition of the three 11–18 schools, a large FE college and the independent sector.

Arden is going down the tubes. We have tried to monitor the situation but we have no mechanisms for controlling intakes and the feeder schools are not playing ball. The effect on the morale of the teachers and on the examination results have been very serious. Elsewhere in the city competition is getting unhealthy. The institutions are duplicating courses at a cash price we cannot afford. (CEO)

From July 1983 discussion began about the development of the tertiary system. In the autumn of 1984 the officers produced a report for committee to consult, on the need for further reorganization to implement full tertiary colleges. The saga continued.

A concluding analysis

In chapter 1 we introduced a framework of analysis which could help explain and make sense of reorganization planning. Decision-making about reorganization has to be interpreted as a struggle between potentially competing groups in which the resulting decisions and plans reflect the greater power of some to impose their values and interests.

An extensive range of actors was involved in Manchester's reorganization, including teacher associations, parents' groups and the churches as well as the LEA and central government. At the centre of the transactions were two interrelated struggles: between the LEA and a local parent group, CREEM; and between the LEA and central government.

These key actors pursued distinctively different purposes. The LEA's principal objective was to devise a system which ensured that educational opportunities would be provided equally to all the young people for whom they had statutory responsibility. For them, only by planning a unitary system of institutions could all students have an equal access to similar curricular opportunities and staffing standards. CREEM's objective was to protect a number of specific schools, especially in the south of the city, which had larger, and sometimes academically successful, sixth forms. The LEA tacitly acknowledged the underachievement of its 11–18 schools: academically, for 18-year-olds, but also in the narrowness of the educational offering, especially for 16- to 19-year-olds. A more effective education required a reorganization which would provide the conditions both for more academic achievement but also for more comprehensive and integrated educational opportunities.

Those committed to developing and reforming comprehensive education in the interests of all were opposed by those committed to resisting change in the interests of some. Public and general interest was opposed by private and particular interest.

The strategies of the key protagonists involved forming alliances and undermining any support for their rivals. The LEA won the support of the teachers and the deprived inner city working class. This alliance was not easily established. The teacher associations initially were opposed but were persuaded by the unacceptability of large split-site schools in the inner city. 'Negotiations' strengthened commitment by conceding a preponderance of sixth form college posts to the teachers, and

The Politics of Reorganizing Schools

Ducie High School to the inner city working-class and Afro-Caribbean interests. The LEA also sought to gain the allegiance of Whitehall officials and ministers in Westminster. Initial tacit support, however, could never amount to formal allegiance. In any event at the moment when the secretary of state Mark Carlisle looked as if he was unwilling to reject Manchester's proposal, he was replaced. This implied a shift in the balance of power and values in Westminster. The emerging cross-party consensus in favour of post-16 colleges was broken by interests committed to the academic values of the traditional sixth form. The first public arena for this struggle was the Macfarlane Committee where sections of the final report had to be redrafted to provide more support for sixth forms. The second arena would be the decision on Manchester's reorganization plans. The shift in power at Westminster suggested a more politicized and competitive context for Manchester's decision-making.

The power base of CREEM was located in more advantaged working- and middle-class interests in the south of the city, and its leaders included members from the world of banking and higher education. This parental interest group forged alliances with local opposition parties, especially the leader of the Conservative's education group, and the Conservative MP for Wythington. The values asserted by this alliance – of parental choice, school sixth forms and acadamic standards – were aligned with those of the new dominant group of education ministers. Informal meetings between London and Manchester strengthened the force of the Conservative lobby upon ministers: 'I fed the local MP with advice and statistics which he was able to use in Westminster' (Conservative education leader).

Thus two alliances began to oppose each other along a number of dimensions: central and local government, Conservative and Labour.

The protagonists mobilized their 'resources' to secure the subordination and dependency of their opponents. The LEA had 'exchanged' resources (posts and a school) to consolidate its alliance. The national education press offered support. The LEA used the submission (section 12) procedures (creating one public notice) to strengthen its case. The LEA, as a statutory authority in the system of education government, arrived at a view about how it wished to proceed.

But these were flimsy resources when posed against an alliance the government was willing to support. The government had used its ultimate resource by preparing legislation – the 1980 Education Act – which enabled the secretary of state to intervene and make reasonable modifications (as well as reject) an LEA's proposals. These powers were deployed indirectly in the Manchester decision in an elaborate dance of 'negotiations'. The secretary of state rejected the proposals although he wanted, it was purported, to modify them. Legal opinion, however, may have suggested that if ministers wished to withdraw three schools from the scheme this would not have been supported in court (because it would have been deemed unreasonable). Skilful LEA officers correctly interpreted the hidden messages and persuaded councillors to accept the modifications which ministers were indicating they wanted. A settlement was 'negotiated'.

The politics of Manchester's reorganization are significant, not just because they illustrate experiences which other LEAs have encountered. From the first, Manchester was regarded, by Westminster as well as the world of local government, as forming a potential model for the purpose and process of reorganising schools during the period of falling rolls:

> Manchester is significant indeed. It is very important to us as the first 16–19, second stage reorganization. It is the lead authority. Many will take to their tents if the Manchester scheme is rejected or broken up. (DES senior official)

> If Manchester goes tertiary the nation will go tertiary. (local Conservative councillor)

> We are waiting for Manchester. (an LEA officer)

The actors believed that the Manchester reorganization was of national significance. The authority's decision, it was contended, would influence reorganization planning across the country for a decade to come. The significance of the outcome was reflected in the intensity of the struggle at national and local levels. And so was the fate of some key actors. Perhaps a secretary of state and a chief education officer were casualties of the power struggle which surrounded the Macfarlane Committee and the Manchester reorganization.

Yet although Manchester did not exemplify the model for post-16 institutional change that a number of education notables had intended, it did, *de facto*, establish new the 'rules of the game' between central and local government in the planning of reorganizations. It is these wider patterns of government and politics that are considered in the next chapter.

Chapter 5

Analysing the changing politics and government of reorganizations

What interpretation can be given to the reversal of plans in Manchester and Birmingham; the interminable delays in reaching a decision about Gloucester city; the deadlock in Newham and Liverpool; inertia in Hereford and Worcester; the inconsistency of accepting York and rejecting Sherborne; of approving Stockport and tampering with Sheffield; and what sense can be made of the most meticulous planning in Manchester juxtaposed with continuing and corrosive uncertainty? Arguably, the period of the 1980s reorganization is characterized by greater disorder and meddling than the episode of the 1960s. How do we interpret such events, which seem to make little sense?

It requires analysis of the shifting politics and government of educational decision-making. In this chapter an analysis is undertaken which seeks to make clear the changing procedures and administration of institutional reorganization in terms of the dominant values and power relations of the period. The stages of institutional reorganization can be interpreted by exploring the changing pattern of values, organization and power within the government of education.

Two sets of competing values have been central to this issue during the post-war period:

(i) the competing *educational values* of using institutional change either to extend equal opportunities or to extend selection and 'differentiation' of ability;

		EDUCATIONAL VALUES	
		Equal Opportunities	Selection/Differentiation
GOVERNMENTAL VALUES	Comprehensive legislation Planning	* 1976 Education Act Report (Secondary Tripartism) (Social planning/ partnership)	1943 Norwood * (Secondary Tripartism) (Administrative control) * 1980 Macfarlane Report (Tertiary Tripartism)
	Laissez-Faire	Circular 10/65 * (Persuasion)	* 1980 Education Act (Hierarchies and markets) * 1988 Education Act

Figure 1 Types of government of reorganization

Analysis

(ii) the competing *governmental values* of planning change or not intervening in the course of change (*laissez-faire*).

If these two dimensions are juxtaposed in a matrix it is possible to identify different forms of organization and power in government of institutional reorganization, as in Figure 1. The early postwar patterns will be discussed before an analysis is presented of the emerging form of politics and government of reorganization in response to falling school rolls. The analysis will begin by focusing upon the rules and procedures for reorganising schools: the way that governments have interpreted these rules reveals both their educational values and defines the relative power of the different actors involved in reorganization.

From administrative control to persuasion: 1945 to the early 1970s

Rules can condense purposes and relations and thus are selective upon policy (cf. Offe, 1974; Lukes, 1974). This structuring of purpose and power through rules is nicely illustrated in the procedures of institutional reorganization which have changed, sometimes subtly, during the postwar period: the changes illustrate different educational values. Those who wish to reorganize schools so as to enlarge and equalize educational opportunities will typically propose a development plan (or scheme) for all schools, embracing admissions policies, catchment areas, staffing and curriculum. Comprehensive education proposes a design for a local education authority as a whole. Those on the other hand who wish to select and differentiate young people will typically be oriented to support and protect the interests of particular schools. Section 11 of the 1944 Education Act, Circular 10/65 and the Education Act of 1976 all reinforce the development plan principle. Section 13 of the 1944 Act, section 12 of the 1980 Act and the clauses on admissions in the 1988 Education Act reinforce the focus upon individual schools. The different procedures operate selectively upon policy and relations of influence. These patterns of procedure, power and values need to be elaborated further during each period of institutional change, of establishing secondary schools and comprehensive reorganization. The discussion of these periods can help illuminate the present changes.

ESTABLISHING SECONDARY SCHOOLS AFTER 1945: PLANS FOR ADMINISTRATIVE CONTROL

The 1944 Education Act 'was aimed at radical change' (Halsey, Heath and Ridge, 1980). It was committed to the values of expanding education and establishing universal secondary education for all. Key clauses in the act arguably gave the Minister of Education important powers to ensure the establishing of new secondary schools 'under his control and direction':

(i) Section 11 required every LEA to produce a development plan of the needs for institutional provision for the whole LEA;
(ii) Section 12 enshrined the plan in a development order which the LEA had to follow and from which it could not depart;
(iii) Section 13 specified how an LEA could tinker with its system (clearly there would have to be occasional changes) by submitting proposals to the minister.

The initial conception of the legislation was of one which would 'create a national system locally administered'. Things did not quite work out as the drafters of the act intended. A number of LEAs produced a development plan but not a single development order was ever made. The rapidity of postwar change denied the plans any total relevance. In the absence of sections 11 and 12 the constitutional procedure for establishing or reorganising schools fell upon section 13.

Section 13 of that Act stated that if an LEA wished to open or 'establish' (or discontinue or, as later amended, significantly change) a school, then the LEA should submit its proposals to ministers and, at the same time, publish notices of the proposals in the local community. If within three months members of the public chose to object to the LEA's plans then it was up to the minister to decide whether or not to approve the proposals. The implications of the procedures were quite clear for the roles of central and local government. The initiative lay with the LEA. It was for them to make proposals for changing the character of schools. The ministers could not

Analysis

initiate change but only react to the proposals of LEAs and could only accept or reject them. They had no powers of negotiating or modifying the proposals. The LEA initiated, the public disputed (if they wished) and the minister arbitrated;

> S. 13 is a mechanism by which the LEAs (re)organize their schools, taking account and involving local opinion (through the statutory means of objection rather than consultation) with ministers acting as a long stop judge. (DES official)

The powers conferred on the centre by section 13 were powers of approval. They suggested that the appopriate role of the Minister of Education was 'quasi-judicial'. The minister would act as a court of appeal when reorganization plans led to disagreement between councillors, teachers and parents. When the local partners fell out they would have to depend upon a minister for a detached, disinterested judgement about the educational value of a proposal.

Such powers can seem considerable but are limited in reality, setting a framework for transactions between the partners:

> These legal powers of central government are familiar and appear frequently in the textbooks, creating an impression of a powerful central government with a formidable battery of controls. Yet when one scrutinises the legal provisions it seems that what is provided for the centre is a general legal framework in which more specific administrative and political pressures can operate. (Jones, 1979, p.30)

For most of the early postwar period, at least until the early 1960s, it is appropriate to call the role adopted by ministers as 'adjudicatory' in relation to reorganization proposals from LEAs.

CIRCULAR 10/65: PROCEDURES FOR PERSUADING COMPREHENSIVE REORGANIZATION

This phase, especially during the 1960s, saw an alliance between central and local government based upon broad agreement about the objectives of (comprehensive) reorganization (cf. Kogan, 1978) as well as upon procedure. Circular 10/65, for example, initiated a new two-stage planning procedure for institutional reorganization (cf. Ranson, 1985).

The Politics of Reorganizing Schools

The initiative rested with the LEA, which was requested to produce a 'scheme' (a development plan) for the reorganization of all its schools; this would be submitted to and vetted by DES officials who would visit the LEA to discuss the scheme's implementation. All was entirely non-statutory and based only upon a circular. The process of approval was internal and unofficial, and based upon private discussions between the centre and the LEA. Only when it came to implementing the approved schemes were the section 13 (of the 1944 Education Act) procedures formally activated, as if there had been no prior consultations, discussions or planning. Notices proposing changes were then published about individual schools and parents were allowed to object, but only about particular schools. The planning system initiated by 10/65 and formalized by the 1976 Education Act established the importance of the department and the LEA as the principal actors in the reorganization of schools. Although the processes of submission and approval under 10/65 allowed the secretary of state to amend schemes as he or she wished, the influence of the centre was to reinforce the principles underlying comprehensive reorganization while the LEA became the central planning authority.

This phase of reorganization saw a relationship between dominant values, organization and procedure in the government of education. The commitment to expand educational opportunities pointed to the importance of planning and encouraged partnership between central and local government. The role of the DES was in promoting (Griffith, 1966) the values of comprehensive education which had begun to be developed successfully in a few pioneering LEAs such as Middlesex, Coventry and the West Riding. The emphasis in this period was upon decentralized, professional, planning within broadly agreed political objectives. Politicians sanctioned the key resource of informed expertise in planning systems of educational opportunity for all. Initiative lay with the LEA rather than the DES. Parents and the public stood at the periphery.

However, when Mrs Thatcher became Secretary of State for Education in 1970 she introduced Circular 10/70, which replaced 10/65. She stated that she did not want to receive unstatutory schemes of reorganization. The formal argument against the 10/65 planning arrangements was that they were

Analysis

unconstitutional. Proposals for reorganization should be presented statutorily school by school. This stress on individual schools reasserted the paramouncy of section 13, which allowed for parental and public objections at the planning stage.

The effect of placing section 13 at the centre of the reorganization stage is to reduce the status of the LEA and establish a closer alliance between the secretary of state and parents. The powers of the secretary of state under section 13, when compared to those provided by 10/65 and the 1976 Act, appear to be considerably reduced, the former providing powers only to reject proposals rather than to amend or to modify. On the other hand, whereas 10/65 made it difficult for a secretary of state to discriminate between schools or areas of an LEA, reorganizing on a school by school basis using section 13 alone could allow a secretary of state to apply different principles, and thus undermine the comprehensiveness of individual schools and the overall system of schools. David discusses the consequences of Circular 10/70:

> One of the first actions of the Tory Government in 1970 was to change, by what appeared to be minor amendments, the pattern of comprehensive education. This dramatically altered the relationship between parents and the state. The government rescinded Circular 10/65 and replaced it with Circular 10/70 which set out the new procedures for the approval of plans for the reorganization of secondary education. The basic change was that plans would not be considered LEA by LEA but school by school ... This Tory change of procedure therefore allowed parents to compete with each other over the system of local schooling. (David, 1980, p.188)

This understanding of the effect of procedures on the implementation of comprehensive reorganization together with the growing conflict between a Labour government and Conservative local authorities over the educational value of comprehensive schools caused Labour, when returned to power in 1974, to begin preparing legislation (the 1976 Education Act). The act would return initiative and control to central government in systematically planning a national system of comprehensive education in partnership, wherever possible, with LEAs.

The Politics of Reorganizing Schools

The election in 1979 of a Conservative government saw the 1976 Act repealed. A considerable shift in the balance of power allowed parents, and especially the secretary of state, to strengthen their ownership of strategic resources at the expense of the LEA. Once more the emphasis in reorganization procedures was on the individual school rather than on planning a system of schools. The strategic actions of parent groups need to be explored on the one hand, and of ministers on the other, in order to make sense of the changing forms of organization and procedure in the government of institutional reorganization.

Changing balance of power from the mid-1970s

MINISTERIAL ASSERTION AND THE SEARCH FOR CONTROL

During the 1960s the initiative lay with the LEA. From the mid-1970s the DES began to reassert its authority and sought to recover control of the service (Ranson and Tomlinson, 1986; Salter and Tapper, 1981). In the field of institutional reorganization this meant a transformation in the role of the Department. To understand this the change in procedures between central and local government for reorganizing schools need to be examined.

By the 1970s, ministers of either main party wanted to initiate change and to ensure its implementation, if necessary in spite of opposition, from local government. The battery of strategies and instruments ministers have used to implement their policies have been described elsewhere (Ranson, 1985). They include the strategies of persuasion, promoting policy in speeches and statements; forming policy planning committees with local government councillors and officers; and issuing procedural advice to LEAs that provide practical help about the methods and procedures necessary for reorganising institutions. A further set of strategies implied more direct pressure upon local authorities: in Circular 2/81 LEAs were requested to provide the department with information on surplus capacity ('Knowledge about the education service is a source of power and influence to the DES', said an official). The pressure upon LEAs was tightened, with the manipulation of the finances built into the rate support grant for local authorities: grant now assumed that surplus capacity had been withdrawn.

Analysis

Ministers, however, dissatisfied with the prospect of merely applying pressure have sought to assert control as well. The role of the secretary of state was shifting from adjudication (1950s) and promotion (1960s) to regulation and control in the 1980s. Ministers used the powerful resource of access to Parliament in order to provide the legislative authority required to secure victory in a struggle against reluctant LEAs.

Sections 12–16 of the 1980 Education Act illustrate the extended authority of the centre. Sections 12–13 of the act appear to grant more discretion to LEAs to close or to change the nature of their schools. LEAs will not necessarily have to seek the approval of the secretary of state: if having published notices there are no objections to the reorganization proposals the changes can be implemented automatically. Unless, that is, the secretary of state says that he or she wishes to modify the proposals. The government has retained the right to call in proposals and to veto them in the interests of national policy even if there is a consensus locally about the value of the changes proposed. (All voluntary school proposals still require the approval of the secretary of state).

Circular 2/80 elaborated the procedures described in sections 12–16. Proposals would be called in by the secretary of state only sparingly and then on grounds of implication for national policy. He or she may accept, reject or modify proposals although he cannot modify 'to such an extent as to change them in substance' (2/80, p.6). The possibility of modification is an additional power for the secretary of state – under section 13 he could only accept or reject. The case of Legg v ILEA has established the precedent that the secretary of state's modification should not be able to change the intentions of the proposals. Mr Justice McGarry's judgement stated that the proposal must remain essentially the same. It was the opinion of a senior DES official, however, that although modification may therefore be a limited power for the centre it could nevertheless be a significant one: 'We could still do quite a lot. Most LEAs will have to put up proposals to the centre because of the constraints of contraction and this will place the secretary of state in a powerful position to intervene, shape and modify' (Ranson, 1985). The Manchester case bears out such confidence: the intervention of the secretary of state in this LEA's proposals, as we have seen, arguably transformed its intention.

The Politics of Reorganizing Schools

Section 15 of the 1980 Education Act provided the secretary of state with a new power. It gave the centre the mechanism to regulate the admission limits for each school over time. If a school roll fell 20 per cent below a published admission base line (for 1979) then the section 12–16 procedure would be triggered: the LEA would have to publish notices to this effect together with its response, and the secretary of state then would have the opportunity to call in the proposals for his or her approval or modification. Section 15 is, therefore, in the words of a DES official 'a major addition to the powers of the secretary of state: in this case to regulate the reduction of school places' (Ranson, 1985).

Although the 1980 Act strengthened the powers of the secretary of state, by 1986 there was growing dissatisfaction from ministers as well as LEAs about the effectiveness of procedures in the act. The department desired more control over the pace of reorganization. LEAs, for their part, complained of frustrating delays caused by the department's consideration of their reorganization proposals.

In Circular 3/87, *Providing For Quality: the Platform of Organization to 1990*, the department returned to the offensive of Circular 2/81, stating that in spite of some progress, LEAs were not doing enough to rationalize their schools to eliminate surplus capacity:

> There will be two million surplus places in primary and secondary schools by 1991, costing some £280 million a year if steps aren't taken to cut capacity ... 780,000 secondary places need to go to save £200 million ... radical steps will be needed ... involving closures and amalgamations. (Circular 2/81)

The circular used the traditional strategies of the centre: persuasion, promotion and pressure. But the intended instruments of control (the 1980 Act) were not providing the desired solution, that of accelerating institutional rationalization. The DES sought to strengthen its steering capacity and commissioned a review of the section 12–16 procedures.

The Mitchell Report (1986) found the existing procedures to be 'slow, cumbersome and expensive especially in comparison to reorganization in the private sector: these procedures are,

Analysis

therefore, difficult to reconcile with the pressing need for reorganization' (p.4). Furthermore the procedures allowed LEAs to approach reorganization piecemeal 'without necessarily working out a positive long term strategy', and they forced the DES into an entirely reactive position in which it was unable to initiate proposals. Moreover the procedures were expensive and did not discriminate between those proposals which were essentially of central (national) concern from those which are essentially of local concern, as had been recommended in the government's white paper, 'Central government controls over local authorities' (Cmnd. 7634, 1979).

It is this latter consideration which was the focus of Mitchell's recommendations. Legislative regulations should be the instrument of government policy and purpose. Mitchell interpreted the legitimate purpose of central control over reorganization proposals as being:

(a) to enable the Secretary of State to carry out his duty 'to secure the effective execution by local authorities, under his control and direction of the national policy for providing an effective service in every area';
(b) to ensure that LEAs carry out their statutory duty 'to secure that there shall be available for their area sufficient schools in number, character and equipment to afford all pupils opportunities for education';
(c) to maintain an appropriate balance in the provision of county and voluntary schools in each area. (p.2)

Existing legislative provision (sections 12–16) had not entirely enabled these procedures to be realized. Central control was necessary, Mitchell argued, but should be limited to appropriate purposes. To this end he recommended that a distinction should be made between 'major' and 'minor' proposals.

Central control should be 'restricted' to major proposals that involve national policy. For example, proposals involving capital expenditure over £2 million; the starting or ending of sixth form provision in any school or single-sex education in any school; the starting or ending of selection for secondary education; and the closure of primary schools more than 5 miles, and of secondary schools more than 10 miles, away from the receiving school. For such major proposals only, the secretary of state would have a general power of approval: if he considered that the proposals needed to be substantially changed it is open to him ... to reject them and to tell the proposers that he is willing to consider alternative proposals (p.13). Mitchell proposed that the secretary of state should have new powers to impose conditions on approval, for example, 'to meet points raised by objectors or to ensure that effect be given to the government's education policy' (p.13).

Minor proposals, Mitchell recommended, should be entirely devolved to local control, which would be within the spirit of the 1979 white paper and of the Audit Commission's (1986) recommendations. The government's concern as far as minor proposals went would be to ensure proper consultation procedures were used by LEAs and that, accordingly, the DES should draw up a code of practice to be followed by LEAs and governors. For voluntary schools, as in the case of county schools, the secretary of state should prescribe the kinds of proposals that would require his approval.

The effect of these recommendations would have been, in most cases, to have considerably strengthened the department, which then could have negotiated and controlled major development plans such as Manchester's. It would have restored the 1960s style of negotiation of a development plan but have provided the centre with the initiative and the control. Yet the emphasis upon *planning* local systems of education ran counter to emerging Conservative Party policy, which was committed to *laissez faire* and consumer choice. The idea of development planning would have reinforced the LEA, albeit in a subordinate role, whereas the new politics of the Right sought to strengthen the consumer and the state at the expense of the LEA.

THE ASSERTION OF PARENTAL INTERESTS IN THE COURTS

While some parents were active in pressure groups during the period of comprehensive reorganization, generally their influence was marginal. LEA consultation with parents was limited and councillors and officers typically had little enthusiasm for involving parents seriously in the policy process. Any attempts by parents to bring pressure to bear through the courts, James (1980) has pointed out, only highlighted the limited power of parents.

In the 1980s parents have become more accomplished and

Analysis

resourceful than in the 1960s in campaigning for their cause, – to resist closures or amalgamation plans. They have been more organized, hired consultants, displayed promotional skills. They have demonstrated, arranged rallies and petitions as the discussion of the Manchester case study showed. Most important, they went to court. They have been more successful than in the past in gaining the protection of the law. Indeed the effect of legal judgement has been to provide parents with new legal rights, which the courts, through judicial reviews, have been willing to supervise and support.

Significant cases through the 1980s have supported the desire of parents to be fully consulted and the pace of accompanying judicial action has been increasing (cf. Loughlin, 1983; Whitaker, personal communication).

In 1981 parents in the Welsh village of Tirabad won a high court decision against Powys County Council (and the secretary of state, who had approved the closure), in order to reprieve their school from closure. The judge argued that the authority had moved too fast, had not given enough time to consult the parents, had withheld information on school costs, and had refused to discuss the parents' alternative proposal. The judge also awarded the parents legal aid to continue to fight the case which was a significant breakthrough in legal practice.

In 1985 a group of parents in Brent sought a judicial review of school reorganization proposals that were with the secretary of state for approval, and asked for them to be set aside. The parents complained about the inadequate period allowed for consultation, the timing of the publication of statutory notices and that the full council had acted without proper reports from the Education Committee. For their part, the LEA argued the case for speed, in order to get a new scheme ready for a new school year in September 1985 and in so doing make the financial savings that would make the service more efficient. In his judgement on the case – R. v. Brent London Borough Council ex P. Gunning (1985), *The Times* 30 April – Mr Justice Hodgson upheld six out of eight points in the parents' case. He accused the authority of 'grave procedural impropriety', and the public consultation as 'woefully deficient as to content and timing'.

The judgement, in effect, has defined and established the procedures which LEAs should follow in consulting the public:

parents must be consulted when the decision-making is still open; they must be provided with adequate information and reports to allow them to make a considered judgement on the proposals; there must be time for considerable discussion and deliberation; and the considered views of the public, including such reports as they produce, should be fully taken into account in the decision-making process by the LEA and the Authority. The judgement elaborated considerably upon the general expectation of consultation as laid down in paragraph 9 of DES Administrative Memorandum 4/84:

> [The] Secretary of State ... is ... convinced that local people have a right to sufficient information to make a judgement on the need for, and the purpose of, proposals at a stage when their views can influence the final decision of the proposers.

Mr Justice Hodgson established more than procedural correctness: he established for the first time consultation on reorganization proposals as a legal right: if the parents had a 'legitimate expectation' of consultation, 'then they have the same legal right to consultation as they would have had if it had been given to them by statute'.

Interpretations have reinforced the significance of the judgement on decision-making on school reorganization plans. Liell (1985) notes that the DES 'reported concern about the implications of the judgement for programmes of removing surplus capacity and whether a precedent had been set for further disruption in other LEAs'. For Kogan, Lightfoot and Whitaker (1985) the case:

> can be seen as one more move in the encroachment of the courts on the specialist role of the Secretary of State. If the judge in the Brent case was keen to see off the Secretary of State, he was at least a powerful ally of parents and defender of the independence of education committees.

Following the Brent judgement, there have been a number of cases in which parents have been granted a judicial review the purpose of which is:

> to ensure that the individual is given fair treatment by the

Analysis

authority to which he has been subjected ... It is no part of that purpose to substitute the opinion of the judiciary or of individual judges for that of the authority constituted by law to decide the matters in question. (Chief Constable of North Wales v. Evans 1982 IWLR 1155)

The courts will intervene only where a local authority has exceeded its express or implied powers. (Wenlock (Baroness) v. River Dee Company, 1885 App Cases 354)

Parents under a number of LEAs have begun to seek a judicial review as a means of frustrating or preventing the authority changing the character of schools, or closing and reorganizing them. In London in July 1985 the high court granted a group of Birmingham parents leave to seek a judicial review of the authority's plans to reduce admissions limits at Fairfax Secondary School, Sutton Coldfield. More recently, in Gateshead in 1987, a challenge from parents has led to a judgement making it unlawful for the LEA and the secretary of state to proceed with a major reorganization scheme preparing for the introduction of a tertiary college. The judge stated that there had not been a proper report from the education committee to full council; that there had been a lack of full consultation with parents and the public; and that parents had not been provided with adequately costed options that would allow them to make an informed decision about the proposals. Parents were granted leave to seek a judicial review and the central and local authorities were not allowed to proceed.

Whitaker (1986, personal communication) from his study at Brunel University of LEAs and judicial reviews over school closures, comments that judgements from recent cases now reveal a pattern requiring LEAs to comply with correct procedure over public consultation. The main issues so far in these cases have been the rights of parents to be consulted before school closures are decided upon, the adequacy of the consultation process, and the criteria used by the LEA in reaching its decision, and particularly the financial implications. Careful LEAs will have to ensure that their consultation process is adequate both in timing and the information presented to those consulted (for example, after the recent Sutton case it would appear that an LEA should provide copies of relevant officers' reports to all those present at public meetings.)

The effect of legal intervention in these cases is to reinforce the democratic process and to make the authorities (central as well as local) more accountable to the public. This is a development much to be commended. As Kogan and his colleagues (1985) comment, LEA practice in public consultation varies and some leaves much to be desired: judicial decision has had the effect of establishing best practice as common practice.

The political and legal challenge of parental interest groups to LEA procedure has been part of a wider judicialization of local government decision-making (cf. Bridges *et al.*, 1985, 1987; Loughlin, 1983, 1986; Milman, 1986). In the case of institutional reorganization, vital decisions have been made in the courts which have had the effect of strengthening the influence of parents at the expense of the LEA. The LEA, the 'leading partner' in the 1960s reorganizations, also experienced a dwindling of its former authority in relation to the secretary of state, who wished to strengthen the control of central government and also to support the principle of parental choice and influence.

The assertion of parental interest groups and ministers came together to form a new political alliance in the government of education. The values and beliefs of the new coalition of power indicated alternative procedures and organizational forms in a new government of education which is now grounded in legislation.

Hierarchies and markets in the new government of education

The government of education in the 1980s, accelerated by the 1988 Education Act, has espoused a new and radical range of values. These values emphasize that the education system should be built upon the principles of public choice and accountability. Individual parents have an inalienable right to choose the education which their children should receive. The values articulate beliefs about educational achievement which assert that a system that is accountable and responsive to the choices of individual consumers of the service will improve in quality as a necessary consequence. As in other forms of market exchange, the products which thrive can only do so because

Analysis

they have the support of the consumers. Those products that fail the test of the market place go out of business. Education is best provided within strong, increasingly independent, institutions which can offer diversity of choice for parents.

The values of competitive parental choice in a market place of differentiated schools suggested very different forms of organization and procedure for the government of education from those which had obtained in an earlier post-war period. The 1980 and especially the 1988 Education Act have transformed the government of education. 'Open' enrolment considerably widens the scope for parental choice of schools, which can now recruit up to physical capacity without artifical limits placed upon admissions by the LEA. Parents have a determining influence on governing bodies which now have responsibility for school budgets as well as the appointment and dismissal of staff. Parents have, moreover, been granted the capacity to take control of a school. If parents or parent governors are unhappy with a school they can petition for it to 'opt out' of LEA control and become grant maintained by central government.

One of the conditions for an effective market place is diversity of products for consumers to choose from. A number of strategies have been designed to achieve greater diversity of school provision. Schools have been granted more autonomy, not only to improve their efficiency but also to encourage them to market their distinctive achievements. Grant maintained schools will introduce further competition into the public sector schooling, while new city technical colleges will encourage differentiation between 'academic' and 'vocational' schools. This distinction between academic and vocational will be reinforced by regulations. Whereas offical policy in the late 1970s had been encouraging the increasing integration of school sixth forms and further education colleges, the 1988 Education Act will designate institutions according to the courses provided. So even where an existing tertiary college is under further education regulations if it provides mostly academic (A level) courses it will be redesignated a school. The market place, so it seems, must be presented with clearly differentiated products. The regulations would help to protect sixth forms from being taken out of schools and reinforce the shift of policy begun by Sir Keith Joseph. He espoused the virtues of sixth forms of 'proven worth' as providing a standard of excellence for parents when choosing schools.

The procedures for reorganizing schools under the 1980 Education Act were designed to support these values: allowing parents to support schools 'of worth' against neo-comprehensive proposals. By consolidating the importance of section 12 as against development plan procedures used in other periods of reorganization, the act reinforced the importance of individual schools above the system of schools. The influence of state and parents have been reinforced against the LEA.

This analysis is reinforced by Benn who argues that the procedures for reorganizing schools:

> will make it far harder for local authorities to maintain the balance of preference, neighbourhood and continuity which is the essence of a successful admissions system for comprehensive schools, for it is legislation designed to stimulate imbalance not to keep the needs of all schools and all pupils in equal consideration. It is designed deliberately to enhance the advantage of a minority of parents and a minority of schools. It forces authorities, whether they wish it or not, to run secondary education systems with parent against parent and school against school in a consumerist free for all. (Benn, 1980, p.39)

Schools have been placed in the market place and their accountability mediated by the test of consumer preference. The 1988 Education Act has not altered the procedures for reorganizing schools but has secured the principle of market competition in the provision of education, with the secretary of state controlling and directing the terms on which the market operates. For example, the secretary of state can vary the 'standard number' of pupils in order to determine the physical capacity of a school.

Indeed, although the public rhetoric of the Education Reform Act is to increase public choice and accountability, the legislation nevertheless grants the secretary of state an extraordinary range of powers over the education service to support those values. Powers to make orders or regulations now refer to curriculum and assessment, schools admissions, financial delegation, the status and government of schools, and the day-by-day management of LEAs and individual schools. Senior Whitehall officials have often complained at the

Analysis

incongruence of the 1944 Education Act which made 'the minister' responsible for the education service but granted him or her few powers to fulfil this role. Now powers have been matched to responsibilities to enable 'control and direction' of the service. How is this development of hierarchy to be understood in relation to the extension of parental participation and choice?

The centre, it can be argued, has strengthened the principle of hierarchy and encouraged the assumption of market values in order to undermine the position of the LEA as the key partner in the government of the education service:

> Legislation, the block grant system, the school curriculum and the planned reductions in the Government's financial support for education represent, when taken together, an actual or potential diminution of LEA discretion which substantially outweighs the combined effects of the measures taken in a contrary sense. Looking at the education service as a whole, it seems that the DES acting on its own initiative and in the context of more general government policies, is now in the process of expanding its power and influence at the expense of the LEAs. (DES official, quoted in Ranson, 1985b, p.200)

Controls from above and market forces below squeeze and erode the discretion of the LEA. As one senior education officer remarked, what the centre is in the process of creating is a new contract between state and citizen that will erode the middle level planning function.

In this chapter it has been argued that the process of reorganising secondary schools has changed over time since the Second World War. There have been different models of reorganization in which the procedures have reflected different educational values, shifts in the balance of power of partners within the service, with appropriate changes in the organization of responsibilities.

Such variations over time have reflected choices as well as constraints in the changing government of education. In the concluding chapter I shall return to a review of the policy issues involved in the reorganization of schools in order to consider the possibility of an alternative model of government, which would allow the ideal of the development of all to coexist with the newer ethos, in which the public participates more actively in decisions about public services.

Chapter 6

Public policy for the future

This book has focused upon the implications of falling rolls for secondary school organization in order to develop understanding of the changing politics and government of education. Falling rolls raised a number of fundamental questions. Should schools be closed or amalgamated to save surplus places and resources? Should sixth forms remain in schools or be reformed in post-16 or tertiary colleges? Answers to questions such as these have reflected some deep-seated differences about the purpose, organization and government of secondary schools. Should reorganizations seek to preserve the principles of comprehensive schooling committed to equal opportunities or should the chance be seized to encourage more differentiation of schools and individual 'ability'? Choice of values has tended to determine organization and procedure for the government of reorganizations: whether they should be planned or left to the market place of schools competing for parental choice; and whether central and local government should act as partners in managing change or compete for parental support.

These issues show what has been at stake and account for the intensity of the politics, the power struggles, at national and local level — the two often interrelated, as the study of Manchester illustrated. The politics have been about two competing models of educational purpose and government, illustrated in the following table.

Table 1 Models of educational government

	Social democracy	Consumer democracy
Values	the needs of citizens	consumer rights
	equal opportunities	different abilities
Institutional organization	comprehensive	institutional differentiation
	schools as part of institutional system	schools as individual institutions
Government/ power	planning	market competition
		consumer choice
	centre-local partnership	centre-consumer link
	electoral accountability	public choice/ accountability

The challenge for future education policy may be to reconcile some of the values and processes associated with these models. In this concluding chapter these policy issues involved in the reorganization of schools are reviewed, in order to explore the conditions for developing a more appropriate model for the government of education. In this the educational values (of planning equal educational opportunities for all young people) can be reconciled with the principles of good government committed to developing new forms of public participation and choice. The questions follow from the framework established in chapter 1, which proposed that analysis take account of the pattern of values, organization and power in the changing government of education:

(i) Values: is there a responsibility to educate all?
(ii) Beliefs about the learning task: is a good education 'a good schooling'?
(iii) Organization: can the quality of an institution exist

The future

independently of the wider system in which it is located? Does the system make a difference to the individual institutions which comprise it?

(iv) Power and public accountability: does the process of taking decisions make a difference to the quality of local education?

VALUES AND PURPOSE: EQUAL EDUCATIONAL OPPORTUNITIES

For many LEAs the approach to the task of managing institutional change has been strongly shaped by an understanding of, and a commitment to, their statutory responsibility, embodied in the 1944 Education Act, to provide education equally for *all* young people irrespective of parental wealth, power or status. For Briault and Smith (1980) the central assumption is the duty of the LEA to 'meet the needs of all our pupils'. The driving purpose of the Manchester LEA was to devise a system which would enhance the educational opportunities of every child as against a system which would allow some to develop at the expense of others. For Fiske (1979), the need to plan the system as a whole derived from an unshakeable sense of the LEA's responsibility for all its pupils: in his speech to the North of England Conference in 1979 he encouraged planning of admissions 'to ensure that authorities can look after the educational needs of all pupils in their care'. Planning for all was essential to 'make real the 1944 Act's vision of "secondary education for all"'.

Beliefs about the form which education for all should take have changed in recent years: is a good education, it is asked, any longer a good schooling?

DEFINING THE LEARNING TASK: IS A GOOD EDUCATION 'A GOOD SCHOOLING'

Education, traditionally, has been something we have experienced within institutions. Whether it has been the primary or secondary school, the further education college or even the adult institute, we have had to go to educational buildings and enrol or register for classes where teachers taught subjects. An education, in essence, has been an institutional schooling.

In spite of the rapid advance of 'open' or 'distance' learning where individuals can follow programmes of learning at home or in their place of work detached from school or college, it is unlikely – *pace* Illich – that such modes of learning will become the general case for all. The institution – the school, college, institute, or university – will always have its place in the learning process. Indeed, the status of institutional learning is reinforced by the 1988 Education Reform Act. Nevertheless understanding about the nature and process of learning is undoubtedly changing very quickly and the notion of education as something only to be experienced in the classroom has been receding. We learn at home, in the community, and at work, as well as in educational buildings. If aspects of learning are to include experience of social skills as well as practical problem solving, together with more traditional forms of cognitive accumulation and imaginative expression, then it is likely that the settings which are appropriate for such diverse forms of learning may differ substantially. Service in the community, practice in factory and office, creativity in the theatre or the band will all take the student beyond the classroom to gain the necessary learning experience. The isolated school as the single site of learning may be a thing of the past. There is a quiet revolution taking place in the processes of learning, acknowledged by a wide variety of interests in education and training (cf. Hargreaves Report (ILEA, 1984); Pring, 1984; Holt, 1980; Ranson, Taylor, and Brighouse, 1986).

Recognizing that students have a broader curriculum to experience which will take them to a number of sites of learning, the emphasis in the new education and training is upon enabling 'progression' in learning: ensuring that students move from stage to stage in a way which meets their needs. Usually this requires planning and co-ordination of the learning process between particular locations of learning in individual schools and colleges, community and workplace. Newsam reinforced the argument in his discussion of the management of falling rolls:

> [We] must move away from the notion of the totally self-contained educational institution with all the interest on its internal operation. We have to move towards co-operative systems of some kind. In a co-operative system we talk not so much about what this institution can offer, but what can be offered to this child. The co-operative systems we mainly are talking about in ILEA are linked sixth forms, links

The future

between school and FE, and so on. (Newsam, 1978b, p.24).

The possibility of developing co-operation is often constrained, Newsam argues, by the procedures and regulations that are designed for the different requirements of schools and colleges. Increasingly the learning needs of young people require the local education system to be managed as a whole, with procedures which support institutional integration and co-operation rather than frustrate it (cf. Ranson, Taylor and Brighouse, 1986; Stewart, 1986a). Yet the relation of the system to educational quality still remains a contested issue.

ORGANISING EDUCATION: DOES THE SYSTEM MATTER?

Does the nature of the local system of schools make a difference to the effectiveness of each individual school and its quality of learning? It is undoubtedly the case that quality is related to 'school-level' factors. The HMI report (1977) on *Ten Good Schools*, or the Rutter *et al.* study (1979) have identified the importance of the headteacher's leadership or the school's 'ethos' for improving the achievement of pupils. Other studies (Hargreaves Report (ILEA, 1984)) point to the influence of teachers' high expectations of pupils, clear systems of pupil assessment, careful and planned progression in learning across the curriculum and between stages in a school, as well as the involvement of parents and the community. The style of school management, professional commitment of teachers, and parental involvement all matter.

But does the system in which the school is located also matter for the quality of learning experienced by children? Discussion in earlier chapters has suggested that because secondary education is a more tightly coupled system the nature of the system necessarily makes a difference. For example, a selective system which 'creamed off 'able' pupils into a minority of schools would doubly disadvantage the residual schools; they would lose the attainment of those pupils and more important, the effect they had on the achievement of 'less able' pupils (cf. Heath, 1984; Lacey, 1984).

A system of schools which is suffering falling rolls, where numbers are declining unevenly and may change randomly, would, we argue, be certain to suffer an effect in the quality of learning in all its individual schools. The changing numbers will have an effect upon the staffing and resources and thus upon the curriculum offered, while the uncertainty will effect the morale of teachers and pupils alike: the ethos (the climate of confidence and expectations) of a school cannot avoid being affected and perhaps undermined. Briault and Smith (1980) in their concluding analysis of 'Falling rolls in secondary schools' argued for an understanding of the delicate balance between the qualities which make a good school and the conditions necessary at LEA level for providing them; the needs of the system and the institution should be in balance: 'There is a complex interaction between LEA policies, arrangements and provision of resources on the one hand and the policies and in-school management decisions of schools on the other.'

> The objectives of government, of LEAs and teachers must surely be a system of good secondary schools. Not, be it noted, a good system of secondary schools, for if the needs of all our pupils are to be fully met, each school must be a good school whatever the system, whether transfer be at eleven or at twelve, whether post-16 students are in their schools to 18 or are provided for in other ways. It is not hard to recognize a good secondary school. Assuming, as will be the case with the vast majority of secondary schools, it is not intended to be selective at the point of entry, then there might be agreement that it would display the following characteristics. It would offer a well-balanced curriculum to all its pupils, with sufficient choices for older pupils to meet their varied needs. It would have enough pupils for their educational experiences among their peers to be full and rewarding. Its intake would be neither selective, to the detriment of other schools, nor over-weighted with less able pupils, with disadvantageous outcomes for pupils in general, such as Rutter *et al.* (1979) have shown. It will be well staffed with teachers teaching those subjects for which they are well qualified. Teachers' morale would be sustained by reasonable assurances as to their future and by a general consensus as to the curriculum and organization most appropriate to the schools, taking pupils' needs and wishes into account. Since parental support is so important to pupils, the school itself must need to enjoy general parental support. The good secondary school would have margins of accommodation which would ease any earlier congestion

The future

and facilitate movement and timetabling, but not to the extent of incurring maintenance costs which unnecessarily used money which might better be spent in other ways. It would be large enough to support the agreed curriculum and organization without using more than its fair share of the resources available to schools within the area. (Briault and Smith, 1980, pp.234–5)

This argument shows a sophisticated understanding of the complex interdependence of local education systems. The quality of the learning experience depends upon the number and diversity of peers, balance in the curriculum, appropriate and committed teachers and the support of parents. These needs have to be well managed not only at the level of the school but also by the LEA: 'There is a complex interaction between LEA policies, arrangements and provision of resources on the one hand and the policies and in-school management decisions of schools on the other' (Briault and Smith, 1980, p.233). Unless the LEA provides the conditions for effective education at the level of the school – and this means managing the system as a system – then the quality of learning for all is diminished. The obvious basis for this idea is the need for the LEA to ensure that each school has an adequate and balanced intake.

Secondary schooling is intrinsically a tightly coupled system for 14- to 19-year-olds whose learning needs increasingly straddle reflection and experience. In a period of contraction the need to manage the system as a system is even more a precondition for learning quality. To recall the images of Newsam (1978b), during the period of growth educational 'bricks' can be added to the wall one by one. But in a period of contraction it is impossible to remove brick by brick without doing damage to the wall as a whole. One element in the system cannot be treated in isolation from another.

The quality of learning in any one institution, it is being argued, depends on the quality of the local educational system. There may now, however, be growing agreement that the quality of learning is not only influenced by the system of (educational) provision but also by the wider local political system in which it is located. Learning quality, it is increasingly proposed, also depends upon the quality of public choice and accountability. The debate is now about how this should be accomplished. Thus discussion about the (professional) organization of education leads into a discussion about the public and political context of learning: who is to be involved and how decisions are to be made.

POWER AND PUBLIC ACCOUNTABILITY: DOES THE PROCESS OF DECISION-MAKING MAKE A DIFFERENCE TO LEARNING QUALITY?

Because LEAs have believed that the quality of education experienced by young people depends upon managing the relation between the elements of educational provision – teachers, curriculum, resources, institutions – they have often argued that making the right decision about provision is crucially important if the quality of learning for all is to be maintained. Managing the system as a system presupposes planning that involves the education 'partners'. A process which left decisions about provision to chance would, LEAs have claimed, proved disastrous for all.

The recent challenge to LEAs, from the new Right and now from government legislation (the 1980 and 1988 Education Acts), asserts that they have omitted the most important educational partners – parents and consumers of the service – from their decision-making. Yet the government has emphasized a form of public choice and accountability which increases satisfaction for the consumer at the expense of those providing the service.

The quality of learning, it is proposed, depends upon the school, not the system. Good schools, moreover, will perform effectively if they are submitted to the test of consumer preference. Those schools which are succeeding will attract parents. Those which fail become undersubscribed and if they cannot improve should be allowed to go under. The same process of competition in the market place which ensures goods meet the demands and tastes of consumers can be applied effectively to improve the quality of schooling.

For consumers to fulfil their allotted role as quality controllers in the market place they require some diversity of product, information about the scope of choice and the quality of performance, as well as the opportunity to choose. The 1988 Education Reform Act has sought to provide the conditions for such consumer choice in education.

Creating this direct accountability between consumer and

producer is the secret, it is argued, to renewal in education:

> In short, it supposes that the wisdom of parents, separately and individually exercised, but taken together becoming the collective wisdom, is more likely to achieve higher standards more quickly and more acceptably to the public than the collective wisdom of the present bureaucrats, no matter how well meaning those bureaucrats may be. (Sexton, 1987, p.9)

To shift from a producer-led system will take time, but placing public choice at the heart of the system will release the quality which is alleged to be submerged at present under the weight of administration.

A number of LEAs have experienced market forces in secondary education and not always been pleased by the consequences. The study of Manchester in this book reveals the concern of elected representatives and officers at the effect of expanded choice upon inner city schools. Newsam's experience of declining rolls and parental choice in inner London led him to express concern at the likely consequences of an unregulated market-place of parental choice. It would introduce intolerable uncertainty into the children's experience of education. If there was no certainty about how many pupils would be on roll from year to year there could be little certainty about what was provided and how. Pupils would not be sure which group or school they will be located in, who their teachers would be, nor which syllabuses they were to follow or books they were to study. Teachers would no longer be sure where they would be deployed nor how their careers might develop. Parents other than those who believed they were making choices could have no certainty about the education of their children (see Newsam, 1978a and b).

Some LEAs which have willingly contemplated the market-place have been forced to moderate their enthusiasm. A study of 'market town' (Ranson, Hannon and Gray, 1987; Ranson and Stewart, 1989) reveals an LEA openly reinforcing the values of parental choice until the success of the policy begins to empty a school which the LEA regarded as geographically and educationally central to its (unacknowledged) system. If that school were to close children would have further to travel, costs would rise and efficiency decline. Kent County Council ran a feasibility study on using educational vouchers in a part of the county to support extended parental choice. Its report (1978) detailed a series of problems that followed from uncertain and varying parental choices, including teacher supply and deployment, transport and administrative costs. Although the report concluded by being against the value of vouchers it supported 'freedom of choice, the full information about schools necessary for such choice, a right of transfer between schools and subsidized transport where necessary to a chosen school'. Nevertheless, the authority has limited its implementation of parental choice to the parameters set by the 1980 Education Act.

The market-place, I wish to argue, cannot achieve its purpose in the system of (compulsory) education. It will be damaging not only for some of the reasons discussed above but, more significantly, because it can be internally contradictory. Whether the market-place is an appropriate mechanism for every purpose needs to be examined. The assumption exists that all goods and services are discrete products which can be purchased in the market. Yet the market can actually change certain goods. If I purchase a chocolate bar or take out an Austen novel from the library my 'purchase' has no effect on the product, although pressure may be placed upon production or delivery. But my preference for a school, privately expressed, together with the unwitting choices of others will transform the product. A small school growing in scale has inevitable consequences for learning style and administrative process. The distinctive ethos which was the reason for the choice is altered by the choice. Some of the most important writing in the human sciences (Parfit, 1984; Sen, 1982, 1987; Elster, 1983) is preoccupied with the unintended public consequences of private decision—making: with the growing realization, especially in many public services, that self-interest can be self-defeating. It is likely in education, moreover, that choice will not only change the product but eliminate it. Choice implies surplus places, but if market forces fill some schools and close others then choice evaporates, leaving only a hierarchy of esteem with little actual choice for many. But assuming that choice is a continuing reality, is education a 'product' which can be marketed?

If education is no more than acquiring a social status which schools can readily confer then it may indeed be a discrete product which can be purchased in the market-place. If

The future

education, however, is regarded more as an unfolding learning process which is adapted continuously to suit the needs of particular individuals, then it is neither a product nor a process which is appropriate to the market-place. The changing needs of individuals cannot be packaged and marketed; nor can the institution, if it is to be a vehicle for their realization, because it will not be sensitive to the needs of clients. Let the market-place be supported wherever it is appropriate but let its limits be understood.

Whatever the product bought in the market place, however, it is its unique social functions which is of fundamental importance. The market is formally neutral but substantively interested. Individuals come together in competitive exchange to acquire possession of scarce goods and services. Within the market-place all are free and equal, only differentiated by their capacity to calculate their self-interest. Yet, of course, the market masks its social bias. It elides but reproduces, the inequalities which consumers bring there. Under the guise of neutrality, the institution of the market actively confirms and reinforces the pre-existing social order of wealth and privilege. It can be a crude mechanism of social selection, as appeared to be developing in Manchester, with the more advantaged beginning to leave the inner city. The market can provide more effective social engineering than anything previously witnessed in the postwar period.

The market may not be able to fulfil the burden placed upon it. Nevertheless, the intention of governments since the mid 1970s to make schools more accountable to parents is entirely admirable. For too long education has been the exclusive preserve of the professionals. The necessary partnership with parents has frequently been neglected. The quality of education which all desire can only be improved when the role of the public in education is clarified and strengthened. Can a form of government be established which reconciles the values and tasks of equal educational opportunity with the values of public choice and accountability? This is the challenge for the government of education following the Education Reform Act of 1988.

The Politics of Reorganizing Schools

Towards public choice and accountability in education

Reforming education to improve public choice and accountability is timely. In a period of change there is a need to establish a more active democracy. Yet the concept of public participation embodied in the 1988 Act is mistaken and it is unlikely that the measures proposed can realize their chosen purpose.

Consumerism in (secondary) education is not only flawed as an instrument for achieving its purported objectives, it is misconceived as to the purposes of public choice and accountability.

Whereas consumerism expresses *self*-interest registered privately and with uncertain (though often malign) consequences, public choice presupposes some concern for the *public* interest on the part of its *citizens*. Citizenship perfectly expresses the necessary duality of the public domain (cf. Ranson and Stewart, 1989). Public means both 'the-public-as-collectivity' (the whole) but also 'the-public-as-plurality' (the many). This two-sidedness is contained within the notion of citizenship. The citizen is both an individual and a member of the collectivity. Indeed, the citizen has to be understood as 'individual-as-member-of' the public as a political community.

The values of the new government of education need to emphasize citizenship rather than consumerism. Individuals need to be involved as citizens because education is a *public* good: a good, that is, in which we are all interested because of its pervasive significance. It is a good which because of its public characteristics cannot be determined by individuals acting in isolation from each other. Education, therefore, is a good which should be the subject of *public choice*, which is accountable to the public as a whole.

The public choice will be accountable if it reflects the interests of the public as a whole: if it relates to the common good. Public choice that secures wide public agreement will legitimate authority because it is grounded in the consent of the public. If choice is to be public it requires the opportunity for citizens to express their views, for their voices to be heard, so that the inescapably diverse constituencies of education are enabled to present, discuss and negotiate their account. Public choice presupposes public participation and mutual accountability.

What should be the organizational conditions for constituting public choice and accountability? This requires understanding

The future

of the appropriate spheres of planning and choice.

JUST GOVERNMENT

The appropriate sphere for (collective) planning is the institutional infrastructure for a society or community, which no individual can establish alone. Thus the wealth tied up in the buildings of schools and colleges is appropriately a public, collective, resource that should be planned, in consultation with the community, to support the needs of all within the community. Given the inevitable interest of Whitehall and town hall, the proper mode of government is a partnership wherein the tiers of government agree on an infrastructure that would enable educational opportunities for all.

Central government has a more profound duty to establish the conditions for learning. It has the responsibility to protect and support the basic preconditions for personal development and citizenship: the rights and duties that define common membership, work and earned income, health and educational opportunities that are not dependent upon wealth, status, or power. These conditions formed the postwar settlement and are as valid today if we still seek to constitute a fair society. They form Rawls's (1972) foundation contract, or charter, for a just society based upon the understanding that one cannot be a person nor take advantage of liberty unless there is justice. Even Dworkin (1984), who wants us to take rights seriously, argues for the inescapable importance of a just distribution that can enable all to contribute equally to a market society. A government committed to a market society has a duty to enable citizens to enter the market-place with rough equality.

THE ENABLING AUTHORITY (LEA)

The LEA faces loss of control and fragmentation of its institutions: any initiative on its part to plan schemes of school reorganization is likely to cause institutions which are threatened with closure or loss of their sixth form to 'opt out'. Nevertheless the LEA can be said to have acquired the positive role of 'the management of influence' (cf. Stewart, 1986b). It can make its role one of strategic influence in enhancing learning quality and public choice and accountability.

Working within the national framework its role can be to

serve schools and colleges: advising on educational leadership and progress; encouraging clear and consistent thinking; enabling policy planning in schools; helping them to set standards and disseminate good practice; encouraging progression between the stages of learning; making staff development suit the needs of schools and encouraging good management practice at institutional level. In this way the LEA can ensure the achievement of quality in the learning process.

Yet this reinforcing of learning quality will only improve public confidence if the the LEA continually seeks to involve the public at every stage and become accountable to the public. The role of the LEA is to facilitate public accountability by presenting information, evaluating performance, and enabling public discussion about achievement and educational purpose. It requires, for many LEAs, a radical change in attitude to the public and a new commitment to involve the public as partners in the local government of education, if its public service is not to be fragmented beyond repair. Dudley Fiske has anticipated (albeit cautiously) the need for change:

> Formal public meetings seem to me of only limited value in promoting a real dialogue (with the public) for they can so easily be communication in only one direction. Written plans to which people respond in writing are not noticeably effective and the traditional British response of offering to interest groups seats on a multiplicity of committees is not much better. The 'phone-in' programme, the local authority newspaper and the staging of events in shopping centres, supermarkets and pubs all have their place and all are in their infancy as a means of tapping public opinion. What has become increasingly clear is that officers can no longer rely on their elected members to tell them all they need to know of how customers feel. (Fiske, 1978)

Having created more imaginative ways of involving the public, the task for the LEA is to shift the focus of discourse away from institutional structures to the purpose and process of learning: developing understanding of the new curricula and how it can be supported by good teaching and assessment. By encouraging discussion about quality in the learning process, the LEA can develop understanding of the system of education and the institutional conditions it requires. The belief must be

The future

that if the public is involved properly as a partner, understanding of the conditions for learning can follow, and with it the capacity to support arguments in favour of improving the system as a whole (even, perhaps, closure or amalgamation). This belief, perhaps naïve, depends upon a notion that the failure of many programmes of institutional reorganization is the failure of the postwar generation of administrators (elected and official) to involve the public as partners in education in a way that would have developed a shared understanding of the conditions for excellence in learning. Can a new generation enable reason to flourish in local public discourse?

SCHOOLS IN PARTNERSHIP

Schools within the LEA have a vital role to play in involving parents and the community. Even HMI, the priesthood of professional knowledge, increasingly urges the importance of partnership with parents, governors, local employers, and the community, in developing the quality of education in schools. 'Schools cannot afford to be insular; they are part of society and accountable for their performance' (HMI, 1988). Evidence of the educational benefit of involving parents and the community as 'complementary educators' grows year by year: in nursery and infant classes (Tizard, Mortimore and Burchell, 1981); in home-school reading schemes, (Haringey, 1981, Widlake and Macleod, 1984); in primary schools (from Plowden, 1967 to Mortimore *et al.*, 1988; in secondary school tutor groups, parent associations and home school councils (Hargreaves Report, 1984), in members of the community becoming 'coaches' to young adults making the transition from school to work (Bazalgette, 1978). Through such strategies and many more parents and the community can develop understanding of schools and their work. The government's paper, 'Better Schools' stressed the important role of parents in the learning process and encouraged schools to 'reach out and support ... parents' as 'partners in a shared task for the benefit of the child'. The reason for forging closer links of this kind is that 'parents can become familiar with the school and its aims' (DES, 1985, pp.59–60).

ACTIVE CITIZENS

If choice is to be public choice it requires there to be the opportunity for citizens to make their views known so that the inescapably diverse constituencies of education are enabled to present, discuss and negotiate their account. Public choice presupposes public participation and mutual accountability.

The challenge is to open a dialogue between all the partners to a public authority – the elected representatives, the professionals and the public(s) – as the basis of reaching an agreed account about purpose and process. The challenge for organizational development is to establish the forums which can sustain such a dialogue between necessary partners as the only basis for democratic accountability.

These organizing principles and values for an active citizenship presuppose arenas in which citizens can become involved and form the partnership which is a precondition for public choice and agreement about education. The constitutive conditions for an active democracy require extensive consultation, participation on governing bodies and in local forums. Community polling could be developed as a form of listening to the the views of the public.

A learning democracy is one which listens, enables expression and strives for understanding. Its conditions are a charter for justice, an enabling authority, institutions in partnership with the public and an active citizenship involved in and shaping public choice. Such a learning democracy can provide the basis for more informed public discourse and choice in a future phase of institutional change of secondary schooling.

Guide to reading

The reorganization of schools has continued to be an issue since the 1960s programmes of 'comprehensivization'. The best introductions to the issues of comprehensive reorganization are:
P. James, (1980), *The Reorganization of Secondary Education* (Windsor: NFER); and M. David, (1977), *Reform, Reaction and Resources: The 3 R's of Educational Planning* (Windsor: NFER).
The implications of falling rolls for education policy are cogently set out in E. Briault and F. Smith, (1980), *Falling Rolls in Secondary Schools* (Windsor: NFER); K. Walsh, R. Dunne, B. Stoten and J. Stewart, (1984), *Falling School Rolls and the Management of the Teaching Profession* (Windsor: NFER-Nelson).
Essential background reading for an understanding of the institutional issues involved in the period of falling rolls include: The Macfarlane Report (1980), *Education for 16–19 year olds* (London: DES) and the Audit Commission's (1986) *Towards Better Management of Secondary Education* (London). Newsam's (1978) *The Consequences of Falling School Enrolments* (Sheffield City Polytechnic) provided an early and illuminating analysis.
The 1980 and 1988 Education Acts provide the legislative backdrop to the issue of reorganization. An excellent guide to the politics of the 1980 Education Act is A. Stillman's (ed.) (1986) *The Balancing Act of 1980: Parents, Politics and Education* (Windsor: NFER). S. Maclure's (1988) *Education Re-Formed* (London: Hodder & Stoughton) provides an admirable guide to the 1988 Education Reform Act.
This book has sought to examine institutional reorganization as a case study in the politics of educational change. An approach to analysis is developed in M. Archer's 'Educational politics: a model for their analysis'; and S. Ranson's 'Changing relations between centre and locality in education'. Both these papers are published in I. McNay and J. Ozga (eds) (1985), *Policy-Making in Education: The Breakdown of the Consensus* (Milton Keynes: Open University).

References

Adam Smith Institute (1984), *The Omega File on Education* (London: Adam Smith Institute).
Alexander, W. (1969), *Towards a New Education Act* (London: Councils and Education Press).
AMA (1976), Education Committee minutes, *Association of Metropolitan Authorities* (London).
Archer, M. (1979), *Social Origins of Educational Systems* (London: Sage).
Archer, M. (1981), 'Educational politics: a model for their analysis', in P. Broadfoot, C. Brock and W. Tulasiewicz (eds), *Politics and Educational Change* (London: Croom Helm).
Audit Commission (1986), *Towards Better Management of Secondary Education* (London: Audit Commission).
Bailey, S.J. (1981), 'Central city decline and the provision of local authority services: a case study of the education service', paper given to Centre for Study of Public Policy/SSRC Conference, Loch Lomond, 19–21 June.
Bailey, S.J. (1984), 'The costs of sixth form rationalization', *Policy and Politics*, vol. 12, no. 1, pp.53–69.
Bazalgette, J. (1978), *School Life and Working Life: a Study of Transition in the Inner City* (London: Hutchinson).
Benn, C. (1980), 'A new 11-plus for the old divided system', *Forum*, vol. 22, no. 2, pp.36–40.
Birmingham LEA (1977) *16–19 Education Review*, Birmingham.
Blau, P. (1964), *Exchange and Power in Social Life* (New York: Wiley).
Briault, E. (1978), 'Problems and implications, of falling rolls: a synopsis' (by C. Beech) of Eric Briault's William Walker Lecture, 1977, *Educational Administration*, vol. 6, no. 2.
Briault, E. and Smith, F. (1980), *Falling Rolls in Secondary Schools* (Slough, NFER).
Bridges, L., Game, C., Lomas, O., McBride, J. and Ranson, S. (1985), *The Judicialisation of Local Government Decision-making*, Research Report to ESRC.
Bridges, L., Game, C., Lomas, O., McBride, J. and Ranson, S. (1987), *Legality and Local Politics* (Aldershot, Avebury).
Brighouse, T. (1986), '16-plus: a change for the worse', *Times Educational Supplement*, 16 March.

References

Burns, T. (1961), 'Micropolitics: mechanisms of institutional change', *Administrative Science Quarterly*, vol. 6, no. 3, December, pp.257–81.

Carey, G. (1981), 'We want CREEM: not skimmed milk', *Forum*, vol. 23/2, p.50.

Challis, B., Mason, C. and Parkes, D. (1987), 'YTS and the local authority', Further Education Staff College, April.

Cheshire, T.E. (1976), 'Priorities in education', *National Westminster Bank Quarterly Review*, November.

Child, J. (1972), 'Organisational structure, environment and performance: the role of strategic choice, *Sociology*, vol. 6, pp.1–22.

Child, J. (1973), 'Organisation: a choice for man', in J. Child (ed.), *Man and Organisation* (London, Allen & Unwin, pp.234–57).

Conservative Party (1974), *Putting Britain First; A National Policy from the Conservatives* (October Election Manifesto) (London: Conservative Central Office).

Conservative Party (1979), *Conservative Manifesto, 1979* (Election Manifesto) (London: Conservative Central Office).

Cotterell, A.B. and Heley, E.W. (eds) (1980), *Tertiary: A Radical Approach to Post-Compulsory Education* (Cheltenham: Stanley Thornes (Publishers)).

Coventry LEA (1981), *The Education of 11–19 Year Olds: Dimensions of Change* (Coventry).

Coventry LEA (1983), *Comprehensive Education for Life* (Coventry).

David, M.E. (1977), *Reform, Reaction and Resources: the 3 R's of Educational Planning* (Slough, NFER).

David, M.E. (1980), *The State, Family and Education* (London, NFER).

Dean, J., Bradley, K., Choppin, B. and Vincent, D. (1979), *The Sixth Form and its Alternatives* (Slough: NFER).

Dennison, W.F. (1983), 'Reconciling the irreconcilable: declining school rolls and the organisation of the system', *Oxford Review of Education*, vol. 9, no. 2, pp.79–89.

DES (1965), *The Organisation of Secondary Education*, Circular 10 (London: DES 12 July).

DES (1977), *Admission of Children to the School of their Parents' Choice: A Consultative Paper* (London: DES).

DES (1979a), *Aspects of Secondary Education in England: A Survey by HM Inspectorate* (London: HMSO).

DES (1979b), 16–18: *Education and Training for 16–18 Year Olds: A Consultative Paper* (London: DES).

DES (1979c), *Providing Educational Opportunities for 16–18 Year Olds* (London: DES).

DES (1980), *Education for 16–19 Year Olds*, Macfarlane Report (London: DES).

DES (1981a), *Costing Educational Provision for the 16–19 age group* (London: DES).

The Politics of Reorganizing Schools

DES (1981b), *Falling Rolls and Surplus Places*, Circular 2 (London: DES 16 June).

DES (1985), *Better Schools*, Cmnd 9469 (London: *HMSO*).

DES, LAAs (1986), *Falling rolls and size of school*, Report of a Joint Working Group of the DES and the Local Authority Associations (London: DES).

DES (1987a), *Admission of Pupils to Maintained Schools. A Consultation Paper*, July (London).

DES (1987b), *Grant Maintained Schools: A Consultation Paper*, July (London).

DES (1987c), *Education Reform Bill*, Press Release, 20 November (London).

DES (1987d), *Providing for Quality: The Pattern of Organisation to Age 19*, 6 May (London: DES).

Dunleavy, P. (1980), *Urban Political Analysis* (London: Macmillan).

Dworkin, R. (1977), *Taking Rights Seriously* (London: Duckworth).

Dworkin, R. (1984), 'Liberalism', in M. Sandel (ed.) *Liberalism and its Critics*, pp.60–79 (Oxford: Blackwell).

Education Act 1980 (London: HMSO).

Education (No. 2) Act 1986 (London: HMSO).

Education Reform Act, 1988 (London: HMSO).

Elster, J. (1983), *Sour Grapes* (Cambridge: Cambridge University Press).

Fiske, D. (1977), Speech to a government conference, York University, December.

Fiske, D. (1978), Presidential address to Society of Education officers, January.

Fiske, D. (1979), 'Falling numbers in secondary schools – problems and possibilities', speech to the North of England Conference, January.

Fiske, D. (1982), *Reorganisation of Secondary Education in Manchester*, Bedford Way Papers no. 9, (London: Institute of Education, London University).

Glazier, J. (1980), 'The sixth form college', *Education*.

Greenwood, R., Hinings, C.R. and Ranson, S. (1977), 'The politics of the budgetary process in English local government', *Political Studies*, vol. 25, no. 1, March, pp.25–47.

Greenwood, R. and Stewart, J.D. (1986), 'The institutional and organizational capabilities of local government', *Public Administration*, vol. 64, no. 1, Spring, pp.35–50.

Griffith, J.A.G. (1966), *Central Departments and Local Authorities* (London: Allen & Unwin).

Halsey, A.H., Heath, A.F. and Ridge, J.M. (1980), *Origins and Destinations: Family Class and Education in Modern Britain*, (Oxford: Clarendon Press).

Hargreaves, B. (1982), Open University Course D208 'Decision-

References

making in Britain' (Milton Keynes: Open University).
The Hargreaves Report (1984), *Improving Secondary Schools* (London: ILEA).
Haringey Education Authority (1981), Collaboration between teachers and parents in assisting children's reading, University of London, Thomas Coram Research Unit.
Heath, A. (1984), 'In defence of comprehensive schools', *Oxford Review of Education*, vol. 10, no. 1, pp.115–26.
Hewton, E. (1986), *Education in Recession: Crisis in County Hall and Classroom* (London: Allen & Unwin).
Hillgate Group (1986), *Whose Schools? A Radical Manifesto*, December (London: Hillgate Group).
HMI (1977), *Ten Good Schools: a Secondary School Inquiry* (London: HMSO).
HMI (1986), Report on Her Majesty's Inspectorate on the effects on the education service in England and Wales of local authority expenditure policies (London: DES).
HMI (1988), *Secondary Schools: An Appraisal* (London: HMSO).
Holt, M. (ed.) (1980a), *The Tertiary Sector Education 16–19 in Schools and Colleges* (London: Hodder & Stoughton).
Holt, M. (1980b), *Schools and Curriculum Change* (London: McGraw Hill).
James, P.H. (1980), *The Reorganisation of Secondary Education* (Windsor: NFER).
Janes, F. (1980), 'A history of the tertiary college', in A.B. Cotterell and E.W. Heley, op. cit., pp.1–17.
Jones, G.W. (1979), 'Central-local relations, finance and the law', *Urban Law and Policy*, vol. 2, no. 1, pp.25–46.
Judge, H. (1980), 'The sixth form college', *Times Educational Supplement*, 5 May.
Kent County Council (1978), *Education Vouchers in Kent*, A feasibility study for the Education Department of Kent County Council.
Kogan, M. (1978), *The Politics of Educational Change* (Glasgow: Fontana).
Kogan, M., Lightfoot, M. and Whitaker, T. (1985), 'Parents granted a foot in the door', *Guardian*, 14 May.
Lacey, C. (1984), 'Selective and non-selective schooling: real or mythical comparisons', *Oxford Review of Education*, vol. 10, no. 1, pp.75–84.
Liell, P. (1985), 'Laying it on the line', *Times Educational Supplement*, 10 May.
Loughlin, M. (1983), 'Local Government, the law and the constitution', *Local Government Legal Society Trust*.
Loughlin, M. (1986), *Local Government in the Modern State* (London: Sweet & Maxwell).

Lukes, S. (1974), *Power: A Radical View* (Macmillan: London).
Macfarlane, J. (1980), 'The benefits of the sixth form college', *Guardian*, 1 June.
Maclure, S. (1988), *Education Re-Formed* (London: Hodder & Stoughton).
McNay, I. and Ozga, J. (eds) (1985), *Policy-Making in Education: The Breakdown of the Consensus* (Milton Keynes: Open University).
Manchester Education Committee (1982) *New Schools and Colleges for Pupils aged 11–19: A Scheme of Reorganization for 22 County Secondary Schools* (Education Department, Manchester).
Melling, G. (1987), Conference Speech, Further Education Staff College, September.
Milman, D. (1986), *Educational Conflict and the Law* (London: Croom Helm).
Mitchell Report (1986), *Scrutiny of Procedures for the Reorganisation of Schools in England*, Report to the Secretary of State for Education and Science, 6 October.
Mortimore, P., Sammons, P., Stoll, L., Lewis, D. and Ecob, R. (1988), *School Matters: The Junior Years* (Wells: Open Books).
MSC (1984), *Training for Jobs*, Cmnd 9135, (London: HMSO).
Mumford, D. (1970), *Comprehensive Re-organisation and the Junior College*, (Sheffield: Sheffield Polytechnic ACFHE).
Newsam, P. (1978a), 'To plan or not to plan ...', *Times Educational Supplement*, 20 January.
Newsam, P. (1978b), 'The consequences of falling school enrolments: an education officer's view', (Sheffield: Sheffield City Polytechnic).
Norwood Report (1943), Report of the Committee of the Secondary Schools Examination Council on Curriculum and Examinations in Secondary Schools (London: Ministry of Education).
Offe, C. (1974), 'Structural problems of the capitalist state', *German Political Studies*, vol. 1, pp.31–57.
Packwood, T. and Whitaker, T. (1988), *Needs Assessment in Post-16 Education* (London: The Falmer Press).
Parfit, D. (1984), *Reasons and Persons* (Oxford: Oxford University Press).
Pedley, R. (1956), *Comprehensive Education: A New Approach* (London: Gollancz).
Peston, M. (1982), 'Sir Geoffrey's framework for decline', *Times Educational Supplement*, 12 March.
Pettigrew, A. (1973), *The Politics of Organisational Decision-making* (London: Tavistock).
Plowden Report (1967), *Children and their Primary Schools*, (London: HMSO).
Pring, R. (1984), *Personal and Social Education in the Curriculum* (London: Hodder & Stoughton).
Ranson, S. (1980), 'Changing relations between centre and locality in

References

education', *Local Government Studies*, vol. 6, no. 6, pp.3–23.

Ranson, S. (1985a), 'Contradictions in the government of education', *Political Studies*, vol. 33, no.1, March pp.56–72.

Ranson, S. (1985b), 'Education' in S. Ranson, G. Jones and K. Walsh, *Between Centre and Locality: the politics of Public Policy*, pp. 187–206 (London: Allen & Unwin).

Ranson, S., Hinings, B. and Greenwood, R. (1980), 'The structuring of organisational structures', *Administrative Science Quarterly*, vol. 25, no. 1, pp.1–17.

Ranson, S., Taylor, B. and Brighouse, T. (eds) (1986), *The Revolution in Education and Training* (London: Longman).

Ranson, S., Taylor, B. and Brighouse, T. (1986) *The Revolution in Education and Training*, (Harlow: Longman).

Ranson, S. and Tomlinson, J. (eds) (1986), *The Changing Government of Education* (London: Allen & Unwin).

Ranson, S., Hannon, V. and Gray, J. (1987), 'Citizens or consumers? politics for school accountability' in S. Walker and L. Barton, *Changing Policies, Changing Teachers: New Directions for Schooling?* (Milton Keynes: Open University).

Ranson, S. and Stewart, J.D. (1989), 'Citizenship and government: the challenge for management in the public domain', *Political Studies*, vol. 37, no. 1, pp.5–24.

Ranson, S., Hannon, V. and Gray, J. (forthcoming), *The Politics of Reforming Education: Towards Public Accountability*.

Rawls, J. (1972), *A Theory of Justice* (Oxford: Oxford University Press).

Rhodes, R.A.W. (1981), *Control and Power in Central-Local Government Relations*, (SSRC) (Farnborough: Gower).

Rutter, M., Maughan, B., Mortimore, P. and Ouston, J. (1979), *Fifteen Thousand Hours, Secondary Schools and Their Effects on Children* (London: Open Books).

Salter, B. and Tapper, T. (1981), *Education, Politics and the State: Theory and Practices of Educational Change* (London: Grant McIntyre).

Saunders, P. (1979), *Urban Politics: A sociological Interpretation* (London: Hutchinson).

Sen, A. (1982), *Choice, Welfare and Measurement* (Oxford: Blackwell).

Sen, A. (1987), *On Ethics and Economics* (Oxford: Blackwell).

Sexton, S. (1987), *Our Schools. A Radical Policy*, March (London: Institute of Economic Affairs).

SHA (1979), *Big is beautiful* (London: Secondary Heads Association).

Stewart, J.D. (1983), 'Tying hands in the town hall', *Times Educational Supplement*, 9 December.

Stewart, J.D. (1986a), *In Search of the Management of Education* (Luton: Local Government Training Board).

Stewart, J.D. (1986b), *The Management of Influence* (Luton: Local Government Training Board).

Stillman, A. (ed.) (1986), *The Balancing Act of 1980: Parents, Politics and Education* (Slough: NFER).

Stillman, A. and Maychell, K. (1986), *Choosing Schools: Parents, LEA and the 1980 Education Act* (Windsor: NFER-Nelson).

Surkes, S. (1987), 'Sixth-form study scheme aims to beat falling rolls', *Times Educational Supplement*, 5 June.

Sylvester, F. (1978), 'Rights are one thing, choice is something else', *Education Guardian*, 21 November.

Tizard, B., Mortimore, J. and Burchell, B. (1981), *Involving Parents in Nursery and Infant Schools* (London: Grant McIntyre).

Tweedie, J. (1986), 'Parental choice of school: legislating the balance', in Stillman, op. cit., pp.3–10.

Walsh, K., Dunne, R., Stoten, B. and Stewart, J.D. (1984), *Falling Rolls and the Management of the Teaching Profession* (Windsor: NFER-Nelson).

Walsh, K., Dunne, R., Stewart, J.D. and Stoten, B. (1985), 'Staffing the secondary school', *Oxford Review of Education*, vol. 11, no. 1, pp.19–31.

Widlake, P. and Macleod, F. (1984), *Raising standards: parental involvement programmes and the language performance of children* (Coventry: Community Education Development Centre).

Williams, G. (1980), 'A new government's education policy', *Education Policy Bulletin*, vol. 8, no. 2, pp.127–44.

Index

academic learning *vs.* vocational training 4, 6, 14, 15
  in colleges 28–9, 44, 45
accountability *see* public choice and accountability
administrative control 88, 89, 90–1
admission limits 20, 21, 101
  under 1980 Act 19, 20–1, 96
  under 1988 Act 103, 104
adult education 29, 31, 33

Birmingham 40–2, 87
birth rate, falling *see* falling school rolls
Brent London Borough Council 99

Campaign for retention of 11 to 18 schools in Manchester *see* CREEM
Carlisle, Mark, Secretary of State 20, 44, 72, 84
central government,
  Audit Commission report *Towards Better Management* ... 12
  Conservative Party, and parental choice 17, 18–19, 22–4, 94, 98
  Conservative Party, and rationalization 3, 43, 44
  control over LEAs 46–7, 68–9, 94, 95
  duties and role of 6, 119
  increased powers of 7, 24
  Labour Party 44, 49–50, 93
  Minister for Education, powers under 1944 Act 20, 90–1

  and rationalization 3, 10–17, 43, 44
  relations with local government 50, 88, 91–2, 94, 97, 107
  relations with parents 93, 102
  significance of Manchester 49, 70, 72, 85
  Treasury, Expenditure Steering Group (1979) 15–16
  see also Department of Education and Science (DES); Education Acts
Charter of Parents' Rights (Conservative Party 1974) 18–19
citizenship, active, and public choice 118, 122
colleges,
  city technical 103
  county 30
  further education 4, 14–15, 16, 27–8, 103
  sixth form 28–31, 38, 39, 44–5, 54, 80; rationalization of 14–15, 44
  technical 7
  tertiary 29–30, 42–3, 44, 103; in Manchester 55–7, 82
  see also schools
community 6, 8, 54, 111, 121
  see also public
comprehensive education 5, 17, 88
  early development 1, 7, 91–3, 92
  as institutional system 87, 89, 108
  Manchester's plans for 49–53, 57
  persuasion for reorganization 91–3
Conservative Party 4, 18–19

Index

in local government 57–8, 84, 93
  see also central government, Conservative Party
"consortia" see sixth forms
consultation, in Manchester 54–67
consultation procedures, by LEAs 79–80, 99–102
consumer choice,
  as self-interest 116, 117, 118
  see also market forces; parental choice
Coventry 31–3, 92
CREEM (Campaign for retention of 11 to 18 schools in Manchester) 64–5, 71
  objectives 81, 83
  power base 72, 73, 84
curriculum reform 15, 31, 44–5, 104, 110
  see also academic learning vs. vocational training

decision-making see procedures in decision-making
Department of Education and Science (DES)
  Administrative Memorandum 4/84 100
  Circular 10/65 7, 88, 89, 91–3
  Circular 10/70 92–3
  Circular 2/80 95
  Circular 2/81 11, 94
  Circular 3/87 11–12, 96
  Circular 4/82, 46
  civil servants, and Manchester LEA 67–8, 69–71, 84
  expansion of powers 94, 96, 105
  ministers 8, 10, 38–9
  paper *Better Schools* 13, 121
  Providing Educational Opportunities... 14–15
  rationalization policy 4–5, 10–11, 25, 44
  secretary of state 35–7, 42, 46–7, 95, 104; and Manchester LEA 74–6, 76–7, 79; and Mitchell report 97–8; powers 21–2, 73, 74–5, 93, 104–5; see also Minister of Education
  White paper (1979) 98
  see also central government; HM Inspectorate
Devon 31, 35–6
"distance learning" 32, 33–4, 109–10
Dorset 36, 87

education
  government of 5, 6–7, 22–4, 108
  learning process 108, 109–11, 120–1
  purpose of 116–17, 118
  quality of learning 3–4, 111, 113
  rationalization of opportunities 4, 5, 7, 15–17
Education Act (1944) 7, 20, 90, 109
  Section 13 89, 90, 91, 92
Education Act (1976) 88, 89, 92, 93–4
Education Act (1980) 19–22, 67, 88, 95, 104
  and government of education 68–9, 96, 103
  and parental choice 114, 116
  Section 12 89, 104
  Section 15 37, 96
Education Act (1988) see Education Reform Act (1988)
Education Bill (1978) (Labour) 17–18
Education Reform Act (1988) 22–4, 88, 89, 104, 110
  public choice and accountability 102–4, 114, 117
educational policy 16–17
  future of 5–6, 108–9
educational values 8, 88, 89, 108, 109
  learning process 108, 109–11
elections
  general 56, 57
  local 72
expenditure cuts 2–3, 34, 94–5

falling school rolls 1, 2, 4–5, 11–13
  and Circular 3/87 96
  government of education 107
  in Liverpool 34
  in Manchester 50, 78, 80
  quality of learning 111–12
  and rate support grant 94–5
Fiske, Dudley, CEO of Manchester 4, 51, 52, 109, 120

Index

Gloucester, city of 36–7, 87
governmental values 88, 89
 see also educational values
grammar schools 1, 7, 35–7, 41–2
grant-maintained schools 24, 47, 103

Haringey, borough of 37–9
headteachers 60, 79, 111
 see also teachers
HM Inspectorate 71
 reports 3, 11, 111, 121

Inner London Education Authority (ILEA) 110, 115
institutions 44–6, 109–10
 see also colleges; reorganization; schools
interest groups 8–9, 40, 43
 in Manchester 50, 54, 65, 66, 83

Joseph, Sir Keith, Secretary of State 35, 36, 39, 72, 76, 103–4
 schools vs. colleges 46, 47
judicial review, parents use of 98–9, 100–1, 101–2

Kent County Council, and voucher system 115–16

Labour Party 4, 17, 19
 in Manchester 54, 55–7, 79
Leeds 42, 43
legal advice, local vs. central government 73
legal intervention see judicial review
Legg vs. ILEA 95
Liberal Party, Manchester 58, 71, 73, 79
Liverpool 34, 43, 87
local authority associations (LAA) 4
local education authorities (LEAs) 31–3, 34, 35
 and 1944 Act 20, 90–1, 109
 and 1976 Act 92
 and 1980 Act 20–2, 95, 104
 and 1988 Act 47
 and Circular 10/70 93
 duties and role of 112, 113, 114, 119–20
 and Labour Party 19
 Manchester 51–2, 58–9, 66, 83;
 relations with central government 67–8, 69–70, 74–6
 options for reorganization 25, 26–7, 31–43, 44–5
 and parental choice 17, 18, 19, 22, 23–4
 planning powers 7, 19, 20–1, 105
 and public choice and accountability 99–102, 115–16, 119–20
 and rationalization 5, 19–20
 relations with central government 35–7, 46–7, 94
local government 2–3, 6, 8, 84
political parties 41–2, 55–8
 relations with central government 50, 91–2, 107

Macfarlane Committee and Report (1980) *Education for 16–19 year olds* 4, 15, 16, 84, 88
 rationalization 10–11, 13–14, 16
 reorganization options 26–9, 45–6
Manchester 46–7, 49–86 *passim*
 and disadvantages of market forces 115
 interest groups 50, 54, 62–3, 66, 84
 LEA preference for uniform system 53, 109
 as model for reorganization process 85–6
 reorganization plans 39, 43, 51, 52–4; rejected 76–7, 87
 scheme modified 77–8, 81
 schools 61–5, 77, 82, 84
 strategy in decision-making 83, 84
Manchester Teachers Association (MTA) 60, 61
market forces 18, 21, 88
 and 1988 Act 102–4
 limits of 115–16, 117
 see also parental choice
Minister for Education,
 powers 1944 Act 90–1
 see also Department of Education and Science (DES), secretary of state
Mitchell report (1986) 96–7

National Association of Schoolmasters/Union of Women

Index

Teachers (NAS/UWT) 61, 79
National Union of Teachers (NUT) 60, 61, 71
Newham 34, 87
newspapers *see* press reporting
Northumberland 33–4
Norwood Report (1943) 7, 88

opting out of LEA control *see* schools, grant-maintained

parent-teacher associations 65, 66
parental choice 5, 10, 17, 39, 114
   Conservative government extends 19–22, 22–4, 47
   Conservative Party and 17, 18–19, 57–8, 98
   effects of 52, 80–1, 82, 115–16
   see also market forces
parents,
   alliance with central government 102
   as interest groups 54, 84, 98–9; *see also* CREEM
   powers 7
      under 1944 Act 20
      under 1976 Act 92, 94
      under 1980 Act 20, 21
      under Circular 10/70 93
   role in decision-making 6, 8, 107
   role of in education 111, 112, 121
   as school governors 23, 103
   use of judicial review 98–9, 100–1
pastoral care, in tertiary colleges 29–30
planning *see* reorganization; system of schools
Powys County Council 99
press reporting, in Manchester 65, 71–2, 84
pressure groups *see* interest groups
procedures in decision-making 6, 84
   analysis of 8–9, 87–106 *passim*
   LEAs duty of consultation 79–80, 99–102
   lobbying 79
   in Manchester 54–67, 83
   negotiation 75
   and public choice 114, 120, 121
   public debate 53
   public notices 67–8
   seminars 70–1
   under 1980 Act 96–7
   under Circular 10/65 91–3
   under Circular 10/70 93–4
public,
   limited rights under 1976 Act 92
   right under Circular 10/70 93
   see also community; parents
public choice,
   and 1988 Act 102–4
   vs. consumerism 118
public choice and accountability 117, 122
   and quality of learning 113, 114–15
   and reorganization 5, 118–19, 121
public objections, under 1944 Act 90–1
public participation 105–6, 122
public policy *see* central government; parental choice; rationalization

R. *vs.* Brent London Borough Council (1985) 99
rationalization,
   as public policy 5, 10–12, 17–18, 44
   of sixth forms and colleges 14–15, 16–17, 35–9
religious schools, as interest groups, in Manchester 50, 54, 61–2, 63–4
reorganization,
   educational approach 5, 59, 87; LEAs' options 31–5, 44–6;
   and future of educational policy 47–8, 108–9
   institutional approach 5–6, 11, 15, 59; LEAs' options 26–31, 44–6; postwar 7, 121
   plans; in Manchester 59–61, 64, 76–7, 79–80, 81; *see also* individual schools and authorities
   procedures for 6, 87, 89, 104
   role of secretary of state 47, 95, 97–8
   system of schools *vs.* individual schools 51–2, 94, 98, 103, 107, 108

school governors, powers under 1988 Act 23–4

Index

schools 89, 111
   autonomy under 1988 Act 23–4, 103
   closures/amalgamations 11, 31–3, 34, 38, 107
   definition of excellence 112
   duties and role of 121
   grammar 1, 7, 35–7, 41–2
   grant-maintained 24, 47, 103
   independent 82
   powers of secretary of state over 104
   powers under 1944 Act 20
   primary 2, 52, 57–8
   secondary modern 1, 7
   single-sex 50, 61–2
   size of 12–14, 23, 61, 62–3, 112–13
   voluntary controlled 63, 95, 98
   see also colleges; grammar schools; selective education; sixth forms
Secondary Heads Association (SHA) 12, 79
secretary of state *see* Department of Education and Science (DES), secretary of state
selective education 1, 7, 39, 87, 88
   effect on quality of learning 111
   surviving systems 35–7, 41–2
Sheffield 42, 43, 87
single-sex schools (Muslim), in Manchester 50, 61–2
sixth form colleges *see* colleges, sixth form
sixth forms,
   'consortia' of co-operating schools 26–7, 33
   as defining 'worth' of schools 46, 103–4
   falling numbers in 2, 6, 50, 107
   'mushroom' 27–8, 64, 81
   retention of 26–7, 33, 45, 103
   size of 11, 13–14, 25
Social Democratic Party (SDP) 73, 79
social planning 88, 117
Stockport 43, 87
surplus capacity in schools *see* falling school rolls
Sutton Coldfield, Warwickshire 47, 101
system of schools,
   and coordination of learning process 51–2, 110–11
   interdependence of 5, 113
   vs. market forces 107, 108, 114, 119

teachers 4, 29, 111, 112
   in Manchester 54, 59–61, 79, 83
   role in decision-making 6, 7, 8
Thatcher, Margaret, Secretary of State 92–3
travel, problems of 12–13, 27, 28, 33

vocational training *see* academic learning *vs.* vocational training
vouchers, educational 115–16

Williams, Shirley 17, 44

Yorkshire 39, 46, 87, 92
Young, Baroness, minister of state 65, 72